Block Grants for Higher Education

BLOCK GRANTS
FOR HIGHER EDUCATION

Alternative to Bankruptcy and Loss of Freedom

Raymond C. Gibson
Professor of Higher Education

Indiana University
Bloomington

WM. C. BROWN COMPANY PUBLISHERS
Dubuque, Iowa

Contents

and State Cooperation, 63—Functions of U.G.C., 65—
U.G.C. Grants for 1967-68, 68—Data Collected by U.G.C.
In India, 69—General Observations and Conclusions, 70

Process by Which A.U.C. was Established, 74—Frame of
Reference and Process Employed by Murray, 75—National
Problems of Development, 76—University Problems and
National Policy, 78—Rationale for Australian Universities
Commission, 83—Composition of the Commission,
85—Process of Operation, 87—Regular Recurring Grants
from 1958 through 1960, 88—Interview with the Secretary
of the A.U.C., 89—Australian Research Grants Committee,
90—The First Ten Years of A.U.C., 92—Summary of Data
as Basis for 1970-72 Grants, 97—Conclusions, 99—Appendix A, 100

International Problems, 102—Public Policy Versus Univer-
sity Policy, 103—The Functions of Universities, 105—
Organization of Higher Education, 115—The Financial
Support of Higher Education, 124—Increasing Demand for
Reform in Federal Support of Higher Education, 130—
Evaluation of Higher Education, 133—Conclusions, 136

Principles of Higher Education—an International Synthesis,
140—Fifty State Councils on Higher Education, 150—One
Council for Each State, 151—Method of Appointment,
152—Methods of Operation, 153—The U.S. Commission
on Higher Education, 155—Advisory Functions of State
Councils on Higher Education, 157—Specific Advisory
Functions, 157—Conclusions, 158

Foreword

It was a little over two years ago when Dr. Gibson called on me at my office and explained his plan to take a sabbatical from his post as Professor of Higher Education at Indiana University to engage in research, which would hopefully bear out his strong convictions over the past twenty years that our institutions of higher learning should have a free hand in the use and dispersement of government and other grants they received. In other words, the dollars donated should have no strings attached as far as how the money would be spent within the framework of the college or university needs.

I had not had the privilege of meeting Dr. Gibson, except on an airplane, until that moment, but his general ideas seemed to be so much in accord with my own feelings that I was moved to offer the material backing he needed to engage in this undertaking which would, for the next two years, take him to the major private and state controlled colleges and universities, not only in the United States, but to many institutions of learning in other countries as well.

It has long been my conviction that government and other special interest groups should not, by virtue of their financial contribution, gain control of the curricula, the philosophies and the teaching patterns of the schools involved; for, unless these schools are and can remain free from outside pressures in their teachings, then the very meaning of an unincumbered educational facility would be lost.

It is Dr. Gibson's contention that there is an abundance of money for higher education available in this country, but there exists a tremendous waste, since it is not dispersed in the best and most economical way.

He told me that, in his opinion, some of our most famous universities are literally being "purchased" by the federal government, when the vast amounts of money granted them carry with the donation stringent guidelines as to how the funds were to be utilized.

I have long been personally interested in education as a means of qualifying our young people to take on and carry out important roles in this country and in the world in which they live. And if, through help to this dedicated educator, I have been instrumental in some small way toward the improvement of the academic climate both here and abroad, then I shall be pleased.

Albert Pick, Jr.

Preface

The fundamental purpose of this volume is to help legislators in the fifty states and members of Congress to design a sensible plan for supporting higher education. The plan must guard national and student interests and protect the autonomy and freedom of colleges and universities.

In 1962, I was on sabbatical for five months to study the University Grants System of Great Britain. I came back convinced that the system would work in the United States with each state serving as a unit for planning and support. The federal grants commission should be composed of representatives of the fifty states. It should serve as the agent through which federal funds are distributed to state councils on higher education. I believe that federal grants should provide fifty percent of the costs of buildings, operation, and research for both public and private colleges and universities.

The federal government has moved so far in the direction of categorical grants to individual institutions that burgeoning bureaucracies in government and in the universities are now necessary to police the process of grantsmanship.

Research carried out for this volume indicates problems of universities that are of national concern in different countries. I have noted how different governments have resolved the problem of support for universities without destroying their freedom. Successful approaches in other nations have been contrasted with the bureaucratically dominated methods used in the United States.

For example, the most important thing I learned in the University of Austral in Valdivia, Chile during the summer of 1972 is that the University gets 96 percent of its operating budget from the National Government of Chile based entirely upon budgetary requests submitted by the University officials.

It is my hope that state and national legislators and leaders responsible for public policy will find my research helpful in structuring a viable relationship between public policy, national and student concerns for higher learning, and funding of the total program.

It is generally agreed that universities should enjoy autonomy and freedom because they cannot do their work in an atmosphere of repression. However, universities must be responsive to public and national concerns.

I believe that a buffer commission to shield the universities against political interference, to keep public needs always foremost among the priorities of universities, and to present to state and federal governments the financial needs of universities is the best means for achieving fundamental objectives. My research tends to verify the application of this thesis regardless of the size of a country or state.

During the past twenty-five years, the United States has achieved unprecedented quantitative growth in agriculture, industry, space development and education. In higher education, the major debates were concerned with the means of acquiring sufficient buildings and operating funds to accommodate rapidly increasing enrollments. National leaders in government and in the universities have become growth oriented and their focus has been upon finances with only token attention to fundamental functions of education and research.

It is unthinkable that our greatest leaders must divert their time, intelligence, and energies to resolving questions of means, while politicians and technologists fix the goals of higher learning and then appropriate earmarked funds to carry them out.

Leaders in higher education and in government have defaulted in their responsibilites to American youth. Educational statesmen must lead faculties in developing the arts, sciences, and professions of men with vertical and horizontal dimensions commensurate with the problems and aspirations of free men approaching the twenty-first century. This is the challenge to leaders in higher education, and the challenge to political statesmen is to provide the means for implementing a dynamic educational program.

Many of the greatest universities in the United States with long traditions of humanistic learning are degenerating into high level vocational schools under the block-busting weight of our federal bureaucracies. This is not in the long-range interest of America; for the most casual observations of higher education in underdeveloped countries of Latin America and Asia reveal the close relationship between the national control of education, including the universities, and economic, political, and intellectual stagnation.

Freedom in American universities has caused scholars from almost every other country to make a beaten path to our institutions to find the secrets of our economic, social, and political strength. But America is faltering in maintaining that system. Some of our most famous universities are being purchased by the federal government. More than fifty important agencies in Washington have federal funds with which to persuade our greatest universities to place their major emphasis upon science and technology, to the neglect of the humanities and the social sciences. This is happening at a time when the people of the world are crying out for renewal and application of great humanistic traditions.

Government is not the only threat to the integrity of universities in the United States. Foundations and their boards of directors are eclipsing the power of governing boards of many great universities, and still others are compromising their goals to the pragmatic demands of professional fund raisers. These dangers are a consequence of the fact that there is no unified plan for keeping the doors of higher education open to American youth.

Philosophical purposes have been eclipsed by temporary expediencies to compensate for a lack of long-range plans. Every significant piece of federal legislation to support higher education, from the Land-Grant Act of 1862 to the National Defense Education Act, was a response to some catastrophe or emergency. Policy for N.D.E.A. emanated from Russia's initial success in space technology.

The explosion of knowledge has created a problem for higher learning and research closely related to pluralism, diversity and value-neutralism in America. The multiversity is a direct consequence of our failure to establish criteria and standards on what the universities should do and what should be excluded from their programs. The result is the multiversity attempting to do everything.

Therefore it was inevitable that the crisis of the seventies would be philosophical—a crisis of purpose and direction. The crisis in accountability is a result of the failure to establish priorities with respect to fundamental substantive purposes and curricula. Universities have been associated with civilization's most respected achievements in values, taste and cultural progress. But in recent years, they have been noted for applying science and technological to military problems rather than focusing upon human concerns.

Instead of serving as an agent for constructive renewal and improvement of human society, the university is being used instrumentally as an agent of growth with bigness as the criterion of excellence even in the university itself. Not all growth is desirable. Cancers grow. Unlimited growth has created many social, economic and political cancers. Universities should serve as the brain of the Republic to find a way to remove those cancers.

R.C.G.

ACKNOWLEDGMENTS

For the sabbaticals of 1962 and 1970 to pursue this research, and for the privilege of working in a university that encourages discovery, I am permanently indebted to Indiana University and especially to colleagues who carried on my work while I was absent.

Doctoral students in the Department of Higher Education (from 1958 to 1972) have contributed significantly to the ideas and theory that prompted the pursuit of this study.

Personal interviews with officials in governments and universities together with documents provided by them were the principal sources of data for this research. Only a few names can be mentioned, but I am especially grateful to the following: Mr. A.J. Danks, Chairman, and Mr. R.G. Rowley, Secretary of the University Grants Committee, Wellington, New Zealand; Mr. J.K. Kaye, Secretary, Australian Universities Commission, and Mr. Carmody, Secretary of the Australian Research Grants Committee, Canberra; Professor W.M. O'Neil, former Chairman of A.R.G.C., Sydney; Mr. S.F. Bailey, Secretary, University Grants Committee, Hong Kong; Dr. P.J. Philip, Secretary, University Grants Commission, Delhi, India; Professor George P. Pantazis, Rector, University of Athens, Greece; Mr. Ralph Fletcher, Secretary, U.G.C., London.

I am especially indebted to the scholars in political theory, sociology and higher education who have been quoted so much in Chapters 1 and 5. They have expressed great concern over the problems confronting the universities and the American society. Their conclusions are a part of the background for my research and the recommendations included in Chapter 6.

Without the secretarial skills and patience of Allie Miller, Janet Roberts, Karen Davis, and Patti Brennan, endless revisions of the manuscript could never have been made.

Finally, I am grateful to Bruce B. Bartos and Neville Robertson for a critical reading of the manuscript and to my wife, Gertude Gibson, who spent many hours in arranging my appointments in the countries we visited.

Raymond C. Gibson

1

Provincial Approach to a National Problem in the United States

Interstate commerce, highways, railroads, public health, social security, national defense and many other concerns of the American people have been accepted as national responsibilities. They are problems that could not be solved at the state (provincial) level. It would seem stupid, to say the least, to have the super highway stop at the state border or even the county line. Inoculation against smallpox or typhoid fever is not a state problem. It is national. Disease germs do not respect county or state lines. Neither does ignorance.

There is no concern or need of the American people that is more of a national problem than education. Yet, it is treated as if regions, communities, or states afflicted with ignorance or blessed with cultivated intellect could be safely inoculated against each other.

Higher education has become an indispensable instrument of national policy. This fact has been admitted by officials in all political parties and in every national administration since the beginning of the Second World War. In other words, universities are being used, under a philosophy of instrumentalism, to advance the causes of politicians and temporary expediencies of government. Thusly used, they cease to be universities.

No author has more adroitly exposed the basic intellectual and moral bankruptcy of the higher education Establishment than Robert P. Wolff, professor of philosophy at Columbia University. He indicates clearly the effectiveness of phony needs and demands when they are christened with Establishment holy water. Wolff notes that:

> In the classical theory of demand, no moral judgments are permitted concerning true versus false needs, or higher versus lower pleasures. . . . The result is a covert ideological rationalization for whatever human or social desires happen to be backed by enough money or power to translate them into effective demands. I shall try briefly to show that Clark Kerr is guilty of exactly just such ideological rhetoric.[1]

1. Robert Paul Wolff, *The Ideal of the University* (Boston: Beacon Press, 1969), p. 39.

1

In many of the largest universities, for the 1971-72 academic year, the only increase in budget or faculty came via federal grants for programs dictated by Washington. Purposes seemed to take a low priority compared with finances—at least in many departments. Professor Wolff is very critical as he states:

> When Kerr speaks repeatedly of the multiversity's responsiveness to national needs, he is describing nothing more than its tendency to adjust itself to effective demand in the form of government grants, scholarship programs, corporate or alumni underwriting, etc.[2]

I believe that finances should be used, from whatever level of government, to achieve rather than to determine purposes and curricula. I take heart in Professor Wolff's criticism of what I view as our long leap toward loss of freedom.

> When Congress appropriates money for research into weapons systems, counterinsurgency technology, or problems of manpower recruitment, that merely proves—at best—that the American people through their representatives wish to express a market demand for such research. To say that such research meets a national need is to endorse the purposes to which it will be put, approve of them, adopt them as one's own. By systematically confusing the concepts of need and demand, Clark Kerr begs all of the major political questions of the day.
>
> Surely it should be obvious that the academy must make its own judgment about the social value of the tasks it is called upon to perform. If someone asks what right the professors and students have to question the will of the federal government, we can only reply, what right has the federal government to impose its will upon free men and women?[3]

As a member of the Illinois Legislature, Lincoln made a commitment which we need to ponder. He said,

> You may burn my body to ashes, and scatter them to the winds of heaven; you may drag my soul down into the regions of darkness and despair to be tormented forever; but you will never get me to support a measure which I believe to be wrong, although by doing so I may accomplish that which I believe to be right.[4]

Freedom has always been an expensive commodity, and some universities have made their choice between bankruptcy and slavery—a choice between categorical grants and huge deficits, between freedom and bread.

---

2. *Ibid.,* pp. 39-40.
3. *Ibid.,* p. 40.
4. Carl Sandburg, *Abraham Lincoln, The Prairie Years* (New York: Harcourt, Brace and Co., 1927), p. 195.

No freedom is more relevant than freedom to determine purposes (or at least to participate in such determination) that guide one's actions and the actions of his institution. To respond to demands because funds are available to meet them is to lose sight of philosophical purposes.

Ever since Mr. Kerr's involuntary separation from the presidency at Berkeley, voluntary Establishment groups have canonized him. His releases from the Carnegie Foundation carry as much prestige and validity as revelations from the Delphi Oracle in the sixth century B.C. Dr. Wolff tends to imply that Mr. Kerr is no better for our citadel of learning than the high priests were for the temple of Apollo.

> So many of the hopes and fears of the American people (Kerr writes) are now related to our educational system and particularly to our universities—the hope for longer life, for getting into outer space, for a higher standard of living; our fears of Russian or Chinese supremacy, of the bomb and annihilation, of individual loss of purpose in the changing world. For all these reasons and others, the university has become a prime instrument of national purpose.[5]

The words are as soothing as those of a high priestess (year 431 B.C.) gaining consciousness from her mystical seizure and, for a handsome consulting fee, informing the leaders of Sparta how easy it will be for them to wallop Athens in the Peloponnesian War.

Professor Wolff does not believe that the multiversity is a reliable oracle for 1972 even though the words are right out of the mystical vocabulary of Apollo's temple. He states,

> Kerr's voice is the voice of praise, but his words are an unwitting indictment of the modern university. So we come to our last criticism of the multiversity. If it is an instrument of national purpose, then it cannot be a critic of national purpose, for an instrument is a means, not an evaluator of ends.[6]

Hundreds of people who attended the meeting of the American Association for Higher Education in March, 1972 anticipated that Dr. Kerr, as featured speaker, would stand up and be counted as a critic and statesman who might help lead us out of the wilderness. Hundreds were disappointed. He was party to the California pace-setting system. It has failed and certainly failed him, yet he seems determined to spend most of his time and considerable foundation

5. Wolff, *op. cit.*, p. 41.
6. *Ibid.*, p. 41.

funds trying to keep the multiversity alive. Most students and professors, and a few administrators and trustees understand this instrumentalist role to which the universities have been relegated.

The principal cause of the crisis in higher education is axiological. There are no guiding purposes. Values have been abandoned. Everything is situational or relative. Pluralism has degenerated into license. Students have become the victims of their elders' most sordid instincts. They virtually cry out and reach out for purposes that deserve to serve as guides to their actions while spokesmen for the higher education Establishment proclaim that there is no truth—only the search for truth.

Citizens are expected to provide unlimited support to universities whose leaders proclaim at all the conventions that the only truth to which the university can give its allegiance is the search for truth. After twenty-five centuries of higher learning in the Western world, and even longer in the East, are we to conclude that nothing has been learned?

REBELLION OF STUDENTS AND CITIZENS

Traditions that have developed over a period of more than three centuries are being challenged in the largest and most renowned universities in the United States. The challenge is generally triggered by students from within and concerned citizens from without. In most cases the battle stations of tradition are being manned by faculties, administrators and trustees.

The undergraduate student is raising hell because too many college and university bulletins state that he is the center of university concern but act as if he were incapable of perceiving the difference between verbiage and action—between promise and practice.

John R. Searle[7] believes that America is developing a culture which our best men will refuse to honor. He sees student rebellion as a consequence of misused affluency, radical changes in the style of upbringing in the home (a much greater degree of freedom), unresponsiveness or obsolescence of institutions (including obsolete structure of universities), the challenge of authority everywhere, bigness

---

7. John R. Searle, *The Campus War* (New York: The World Publishing Co.), pp. 137-38 and 174-75.

of universities, family and social pressures that tend to force unmotivated young people to go to college, and the crisis in educational philosophy. David Graber, Class of 1969 at the University of California, noted:

> Pericles said in his funeral oration, comparing Athens to Sparta, "We do not say in Athens that those men who have no business in politics mind their own business. But rather we say that those men whose business is not politics have no business in Athens at all." Every citizen has a debt and an obligation to get involved. And this is a dream, this participatory democracy thing, with anybody who's read any politics.[8]

The problem is not limited to the United States or to any one region of the world. In 1970, Mr. Swapan K. Mullick (New Delhi, India) noted that:

> India's student politics is associated with violent dissent, contempt for authority, disrespect for elders and a general confusion of social and moral values. It is for the Government to see that university courses are geared to meet social and economic needs.
>
> Our university courses fall woefully short of this requirement. Our universities pride themselves on being intellectual power-houses. But judging from their indifference to the vital process of changing with the times, they are likely to remain in closed ivory towers for a long time to come. Because they are in a vacuum withdrawn from reality, reality assails their doors with greater violence.[9]

At the beginning of the decade of the sixties, Carroll Hanson, U.S. Office of Education, observed that eighty-nine million American citizens twenty years of age and over had never taken a college course. Most of them had never seen a physics laboratory or a college library. They had virtually no conception of a liberal arts education or the functions of a professor.

The decade of the seventies will be different. Citizens are beginning to know their universities. Unfortunately what they have seen during these years of dissent and destruction has not helped the image of higher education. What they have not seen, and in some respects can never see, are the causes that gave rise to dissent and violence. The surface symptoms make citizens and policemen anxious to club the students. If they could perceive the causes, their

---

8. Art Seidenbaum, *Confrontation on Campus* (Los Angeles: The Ward Ritchie Press, 1969), pp. 138-39.
9. International Association of Universities, Bulletin: Vol. XVIII, No. 4, Paris, 1970, pp. 239-40.

wrath would be directed toward trustees, administrators and professors, and government officials in Washington.

The taxpapers' revolt now surfacing in one state legislature after another is evidence of an increasing educational sophistication on the part of citizens. They believe that higher education is a good thing and should receive adequate support, however, no agency of society deserves a blank check in using public funds. On the challenge of the tighter budget, Bressler has declared:

> The dilemma that will now try the ingenuity of American colleges will be how to improve quality while maintaining or reducing the present level of expenditure. The recognition of scarcity is the ultimate check on our fantasies.[10]

Concerned parents and taxpayers need to demand the answers to some hard questions emanating from research on class size. 1. Why should a college class be smaller than a first grade? 2. Why should college teachers who do no research or writing teach only three to nine class-hours per week when secondary teachers are required to teach twenty-five to thirty hours?

There has been a tendency to equate everything good with the level of financial support. This false god, long a characteristic of government and the military, became the patron saint of universities in the decade of the sixties. Citizens, trustees, professors and legislators who raised questions about the merit of increasing state support of universities have been labeled as reactionary or stupid, or anti-intellectual. Citizens are now becoming convinced that universities do not exist for faculties or trustees or administrators. They do not exist exclusively for students or for the Department of Defense.

The functions, organization, and support of universities are not university policies—they are public policies that should not, and cannot, be entrusted exclusively to the university community.

Indeed, administrators, trustees and faculties are no better qualified to legislate university policies than the Executive Branch of the United States Government is to legislate for the whole nation. The typical state university is too complex for part-time trustees or part-time legislators to evaluate the astronomical budgetary requests submitted by university officials.

---

10. Marvin Bressler, *The American College: Some Problems and Choices* (Annals of the American Academy of Political and Social Science, July 1971), p. 60.

What is called for as a matter of public policy is for the academic community, insightful citizens and political leaders, at the state and national levels, to design a system that will serve the public need. Citizens should not settle for less and universities should ask for no more.

Participation in democracy is increasing in our society, and it would be a metaphysical contradiction for the greatest possible laboratory (the university) in the learning and practicing of democratic principles to be oblivious to the changes or to fail to take the lead. On this point Bressler has written:

> Decision was once the privilege of the wise, wisdom was certified by tenure, and the sages were accountable only to Truth and each other. This halcyon era has been supplanted by the new age of student participation in every major aspect of institutional existence: corporate relationships, educational program, and internal order.[11]

ORGANIZATIONAL ANARCHY VERSUS PUBLIC POLICY

The United States is in a state of anarchy in respect to purposes and organization for higher education. There is no guarantee that the national or state interests are being served. There certainly is little evidence that the best interests of students are being served. Moreover, there is a dearth of evidence of prudence in the financial management of universities. Unfortunately no level of government is adequately organized to deal with these problems.

Most of the leaders in state universities have fought the idea of effective and intelligent coordination of higher education at the state level. Systems that have been established have not had the benefit of insight which the academic community could have contributed. There is nearly always the hidden or acknowledged hope that coordinating agencies will fail. They usually do because of a purely political approach to appointments and unsophisticated leadership regarding functions.

After years of frustration and opposition from state universities, the Indiana General Assembly in 1971 established a Commission on Higher Education. Members were appointed by the governor from

---

11. *Ibid.,* p. 61.

congressional districts. Then the Commission, perhaps with slight prodding from the governor, appointed the governor's assistant as the first Commissioner for Higher Education. Thus, the entire creature is a political rather than an educational agency.

There is a haphazard approach in the selection of functions and objectives which colleges and universities seek to attain. Nearly 3,000 different institutions move in all directions in determining their responsibilities, patterns of organization, and how to finance programs.

Almost every new university president, and there are many of them every year, spends the first year or two, if he serves that long, in reorganizing his institution. Boards of trustees generally take it for granted that a new president will want to reorganize the university. This is evidence that university officials and trustees either do not believe that there are any valid principles of university organization or if desirable patterns do exist they don't know about them. Some of the most distinguished university presidents in America have spent their whole careers in perfecting sensible organizations only to have them dismantled as soon as they retire. This represents an enormous waste of personnel and financial resources.

There is a state of anarchy in the financing of higher education. In 1959-60 the total cost of higher education was $8 billion. In 1969-70 the cost had risen to $21.2 billion. General and administrative costs were $1,820 million while faculty salaries were $5,610 million. General and administrative expenditures were almost a third as much as faculty salaries and represented 8.6 percent of the total budget.

Federal grants to private as well as public institutions, under criteria now applied, have (in the words of some of my students) invoked socialism for powerful firms such as Lockheed, and private enterprise for the poor people. On this point Stedman has noted:

> Private federalism has also created its own new-style pressure groups with an enormous potential for innovative leadership and mobilization of political resources. Private federalism probably tends to increase some disparities between public and private programs and rich and poor. It tends in the first instance to afford opportunity mainly to the competent and resourceful, and to benefit for the longer run primarily those able to implement new discovery and to attract and hold trained manpower. In concrete terms, elite universities and well-established medical complexes, California and Michigan and New York City, do well while others do less well. Universities, hospitals, and professional groups have often benefited

enormously, public programs have often got less, and been out of the mainstream—more in backward states and cities, but also everywhere.[12]

Stedman also noted that the issue of whether NIH will increasingly become a health rather than a science agency will depend upon factors other than the greatest public good, and the decision itself ultimately in the keeping of a few men, many of whom will not be in government at all.[13]

Federal aid to higher education increased from $2.7 billion in 1965-66 to $5 billion in 1970. But the federal government is part of the problem rather than a solution to the problem of financing, because categorical grants to perform functions dictated by the federal government invariably result in increased drains on operating budgets for ongoing programs which are not funded by the federal government. There is a tendency to employ high level personnel to carry out federal programs, but as federal or foundation money runs out, personnel and added costs are generally absorbed by the university in its regular operating budget. Therefore, in reality the federal government is helping many universities along the road toward bankruptcy and loss of freedom.

There is no organized plan to keep the independent colleges and universities alive in this country. They have been a very important part of the strength of higher education in the United States and should be utilized to capacity as enrollments increase and funds for construction even in state universities tend to level off.

Finally, there is no effective means for evaluating institutions of higher learning. Criteria are needed for determining the functions, organizations, financial costs, and evaluation. They are needed at the state and national levels and they are indispensable to each individual institution. Calvin B.T. Lee has stated:

> More and more, decisions about curricular development, research, specific projects, construction, and so forth, are based on such external considerations as the prospects for foundation and government grants. Universities apply for, accept, and house research grants without adequately checking whether the research supports and enchances the purposes of the university or whether it diverts energies, space, time, and effort from more important institutional endeavors.[14]

---

12. Murray S. Stedman, Jr., Editor, *Modernizing American Government* (Englewood Cliffs, N.J.: Prentice-Hall, Inc., 1968), p. 148.
13. *Ibid.*, p. 149.
14. Charles G. Dobbins and Calvin B.T. Lee, *Whose Goals for American Higher Education?* (Washington, D.C., 1968), pp. 14-15.

A senior statesman who has divided his time between universities, government and industry has delineated five reasons why government and other agencies of society turn to universities to solve their problems. John Corson has stated,

> First, the university provides unique institutional strengths. It has a staff, buildings and grounds, and endowment, and it has more. Second, the universities, as they have grown, have acquired a substantial monopoly of the particular kind of human talent required for dealing with the problems of a society as distinguished from the problems of an enterprise. Third, the universities possess a discipline of objectivity. Fourth, the universities are committed to the search for new knowledge. Fifth, the university possesses values; it stands for something; indeed it stands for the most civilizing values of which we know—freedom, for example.[15]

Now I agree with Mr. Corson on all of these points, but the extent to which the university should be involved in such activities as solving problems of government, of industry, of the military, of health and other aspects of American society is a matter of public policy. I do not believe that every institution should be permitted to go it alone. Moreover, the five great strengths, outlined by Dr. Corson as causing government and other agencies to turn to the universities for solutions of their problems, have never been brought to bear upon the solutions of the problems of the universities themselves.

The objectivity, talent, insight, research, and concern for human values of the universities and their most distinguished scholars must be joined by the most outstanding leaders of our society in designing a scheme that will guarantee that the universities serve the youth as well as the national interest, that they be adequately financed in doing so, and that freedom and responsibility within individual universities be maintained. Dr. Logan Wilson, President of the American Council on Education, has stated:

> We would all agree, I trust, that higher education has become too crucial to the general welfare for its development to be left entirely in local hands. Many urgent problems cannot be adequately dealt with by individual institutions acting unilaterally, and piecemeal approaches do not yield satisfactory patterns. With the growing collectivism of modern life, more and more decisions and actions affecting the present and future of higher education are being transferred from the private to the public arena, and from the local to the state or national level.[16]

15. *Ibid.,* p. 84.
16. *Ibid.,* p. 138.

Wilson discusses the growing trend toward state-wide commissions on higher education designed to do for institutions what they were unable or unwilling to do for themselves.

Perhaps Wilson's strongest endorsement of an arrangement similar to the one proposed in this volume is his statement,

> On all sides, there has been increased awareness of the need to distribute funds fairly among existing institutions and to have an orderly plan for their expansion and for the establishment of new institutions. An agency that reviews programs and budgets can well be looked at constructively as a means for implementing goals rather than as a device for keeping costs down.[17]

James E. Allen, Jr., former Commissioner of Education in New York and former U.S. Commissioner of Education, has noted the increasing significance of federal participation in the financing of higher education. He stated that in a three-year period, between 1965 and 1968, federal funds for higher education in New York increased from virtually nothing to $44 million. Allen stated "The greatest pressure bearing upon institutions of higher education today is government involvement." He regards it as imperative that leaders in government and in the universities "support those policies and programs that help to ensure that the effect of growing governmental participation in higher education will promote institutional freedom and integrity."[18] John William Padberg has stated:

> Institutional autonomy is restricted by federal financial involvement and by accrediting demands. I wonder whether institutions of higher education have the intestinal fortitude and can intelligently cooperate to acknowledge and to proclaim directly and repeatedly two facts: first, that they—both public and private universities and colleges—need unconditional governmental support, either by direct grants to the students or by across-the-board help to the institution; second, that because our government wants and needs these institutions, it cannot, even if simply as a matter of national public policy, afford to let them degenerate. There are formidable risks in making such statements. But I think that not to make them bears even more formidable implications and bodes dangerous results. He who pays the piper does, indeed, now call the tune, but unless we devise some system whereby institutions retain their autonomy and individual characters, we shall all be marching to the same tune; a disastrous outcome in a society that has prized and prospered from institutional diversity.[19]

---

17. *Ibid.,* p. 139.
18. *Ibid.,* p. 192.
19. *Ibid.,* p. 194.

THE ACCOUNTABILITY GAP IN RELATIONSHIP
WITH THE LEGISLATURES

During the spring of 1971, it became evident that there was a catastrophic loss of confidence between university officials, state coordinating commissions, budget bureaus, the governors and legislators. The pattern became a familiar one. Operating requests of universities, in many instances, were cut as much as fifty percent by the time the legislators and the governor completed action on appropriations. Requests for new construction were drastically cut or were completely deleted from appropriations.

These radical discrepancies between requests and appropriations lead to two fundamental questions. One, how can officials in the bureau of the budget and in the legislature, with all the other things that demand their attention, have the expertise and the time to make intelligent reductions of up to fifty percent in the requests of universities for operating budgets and seventy-five percent reductions in requests for building programs? Two, if the budgets, in fact, deserved to be cut and were therefore padded to the tune of fifty to one-hundred percent, how could the public in general have any confidence in university authorities and boards of trustees who made the original requests?

Members of the legislatures and of the executive branches of state governments, the public in general, and the universities themselves will surely remember the 1971 sessions of legislatures as raising serious doubts about the methods by which university requests are developed and consequent actions by state authorities. How can the needs of society and the integrity of universities be brought into harmony?

VOLUNTARY ASSOCIATIONS

The Tenth Amendment to the United States Constitution stated: "Powers not delegated to the United States by the Constitution, nor prohibited by it to the States, are reserved to the States respectively, or to the people." This caused education to develop as a state function. The natural consequence has been an excessive proliferation of voluntary agencies. In fact a conglomeration of bureaucratic cartels with interlocking directorates, boards, and financing has been a natural result of the vacuum in federal authority and responsibility with respect to education. Voluntary groups tend to become special interest groups.

De Tocqueville observed, more than a century ago, that no country in the world had used the principle of association more successfully and unsparingly than America. More recently Diamond, *et al.*, have stated: "Interest groups are important in all democracies, but their diversity and power are particularly great in the United States. An authoritative estimate found some 20,000 national associations plus an even greater number of locally organized groups."[20]

These authors noted the close relationship between special interest groups and the political system that has developed in America.

> Interest groups fragment and specialize, in part, because they have a great variety of fragmented and specialized portions of political power to deal with.
> A British M.P. dares not break party ranks on a significant vote no matter how much pressure the local industrial giant may bring to bear. In the United States, a congressman is far freer to respond to such pressure and, therefore, gets more pressure. The weakness of centralized party power within the legislative chamber entails the increased power of interest groups in the lobby. In sum, American interest groups are both more fragmented into narrowly particularized interests and also more powerful in influencing individual officials than are the organized interests of other democratic countries.[21]

Students, parents, taxpayers, and the general society are the victims of cartels of finance, curriculum, organization, policy, accreditation, boards of trustees, administrators, and professors, plus the 20,000 special interest groups in the political and business arena.

The system of cartels has resulted in all kinds of national organizations with tremendous influence and resources but with no formal or legal responsibility for solving the problems of higher education. The National Education Association has been the principal voluntary organization for the public school teachers. The American Council on Education, the Association of Land-Grant Colleges and Universities, and the American Association of Colleges are all prime examples of organizations of great national prestige, influence, financial resources, and considerable power.

I believe that in general higher education in each state and in the

20. Martin Diamond, Winston M. Fisk and Herbert Garfinkel, *The Democratic Republic: An Introduction to American National Government* (Chicago: Rand McNally and Co., 1966), p. 315.
21. *Ibid.*, p. 315.

nation as a whole is represented before legislative bodies by special interest groups rather than by individuals or groups whose interest is the total society. Political scientists and sociologists have provided empirical evidence and authoritative judgment to support this hypothesis. For example, Dye and Zeigler wrote in 1971:

> Whatever the nature of the goals of the group, an organization is dominated by its active minority. An organization is composed of formal leaders, active followers, and passive followers, the latter group consisting of the majority of members. Actually, leaders accommodate only those factions represented by active members, whose values are not necessarily reflective of the values of most members.[22]

Representatives of higher education have been concerned only for those students who could compete in the traditional curricula. Both the Land-Grant Act and now the community college movement have been reactions against the Establishment and for the common people.

> Thus we find that interest groups do not serve as instruments for the common citizen; they are instruments of the elites in society. In the final analysis the evaluation of organizations must be based upon how well the elites, through their groups, recognize and act upon the best interests of society as a whole.[23]

Education interest groups are perhaps the best representatives we now have of the education interests of society and of young people who seek an education. But we need better representation of the public interests.

Regional accrediting associations have developed into one of the most powerful cartels because they virtually determine the image of colleges and universities across the country. And the criteria and procedures by which they determine that image have long been suspect in the eyes of many objective scholars, administrators, and citizens. The secrecy surrounding their operations should automatically disqualify them as agents of public policy and interests.

Virtually all of the organizations enumerated above get their financial support either from membership fees charged to individuals or institutional memberships. Therefore, most of the cost for operating the volunteer agencies comes from taxes. Moreover, personnel for

---

22. Thomas R. Dye and Harmon Zeigler, *Irony of Democracy—Common Introduction to American Politics* (Belmont, California: Duxbury Press, 1971), pp. 208-14.
23. *Ibid.*, p. 214.

manning the organizations is generally drawn from the universities, and the voluntary organizations represent the universities and colleges of the United States but they do not represent the public interest nor the national concerns for higher education in the United States.

The great foundations are another significant part of the Establishment. Invariably they draw their personnel from among the university presidents some of whom may not have been noted for their success in managing universities. However, as spokesmen for powerful foundations with tremendous resources to dispense they immediately become oracles of wisdom solving the ills of universities on a voluntary basis.

I discovered three former university chancellors and presidents in the capital of one Asian nation supported mostly by the Ford Foundation. All three of them now have the status of a senicure—a position with tremendous status, prestige, reasonable tenure, very high salary, and no responsibility. One former university president among the three admitted that the assignment was a haven for retired presidents and chancellors. This represents an example of the means by which the foundations channel private funds into public programs. I still have reservations about whether the plan is as effective as an equitable system of taxation and the dispersement of funds by a prudent government.

Most of the representatives of the cartels and the foundations have simply refused to get together on a plan for federal participation in financing the operating cost of higher learning in the United States. One reason for this reluctance is the fact that the most prestigious universities are doing very well under the system of anarchy that now prevails. For example in fiscal year 1966, twenty-five institutions received more than $25 million each from the federal government. Seventy-five received more than $10 million each.

Clark Kerr, in his position with the Carnegie Corporation, has not come up with any plan or suggestion for the general diffusion of funds among colleges and universities for operating purposes. His friends in the greatest multiversities would stand to lose under such a system. Yet, they have refused to develop public policy or to support policy developed by others to take care of the seventy to eighty percent of high school graduates who cannot be admitted to their universities.

No voluntary association of special interests groups, and no combination of all of them, can ever close the accountability gap that now exists in the procedures by which public policy for higher education is developed in the United States. There is need for an organization that cannot escape responsibility.

In describing the semisovereign people, Schattschneider was very dubious of pressure groups.

> The notion that the pressure system is automatically representative of the whole community is a myth fostered by the universalizing tendencies of modern group theory.[24]
>
> Organizations are usually controlled by a small elite. Michels' 'iron law of oligarchy' describes the fact that even the most democratically inclined organizations gradually evolve into oligarchies. The oligarchs, who help to shape the goals of the organization, are drawn disproportionately from the upper social classes.[25]

Dye and Zeigler came to some conclusions that point to the need for reform in our representative system.

> Those who are active in interest groups constitute only a small portion of the populace; moreover, they tend to be from a higher socioeconomic status than those who are not active. In short, it is the elites who are the most active in interest groups in America.
>
> Two overriding facts emerge from our study of American democracy: (1) It is a political system controlled by elites, who govern according to the tenets of a welfare-capitalistic ideology. (2) The survival of the American political system depends on how well and how wisely these elites are able to cope with the internal tensions that develop in American society.[26]

The bureaucracies in many universities known as central administration combined with boards of trustees can never fill the gap either because the increasing complexity of the universities and the growing inclination towards systems of higher education mandate that the bureaucracy look first to its own preservation and only secondarily to the development of a total system of equitable educational opportunity beyond the high school.

---

24. E.E. Schattschneider, *The Semisovereign People; A Realist's View of Democracy in America* (New York: Holt, Rinehart and Winston, 1960), p. 35.
25. Robert Michels, *Political Parties: A Sociological Study of the Oligarchical Tendencies of Modern Democracy* (New York: Dover, 1959), p. 248.
26. Dye and Zeigler, *op. cit.,* p. 198.

THE ESTABLISHMENT IN ACTION

In 1962, the Board of Regents for Higher Education in Kansas employed Dr. Alvin C. Eurich and a panel of experts to prepare a report on future needs of higher education in Kansas and to make recommendations to the Board of Regents on methods of improving and developing education beyond the high school.

One of the most controversial recommendations of the report dealt with the municipal university of Wichita located in the largest metropolitan center in Kansas. Dr. Eurich and his panel recommended that the University of Kansas and Kansas State University jointly establish the State Universities Center at Wichita under a new board responsible to the Board of Regents. Eurich's report stated:

> This Center, if established with the present facilities of the University of Wichita and expanded in the future under the jurisdiction of the two state universities could: (1) provide for the needs of the college-bound students in Sedgwick and surrounding counties, a growing population area; (2) reduce waste and duplication of facilities and resources now and in the future; (3) draw upon the faculties and other resources of the two universities in developing its program.[27]

Mr. Eurich stated further that he believed that the Center as recommended by his panel would conserve academic resources and offer quality college education and at the same time permit the state to continue its effort to build two great universities with outstanding faculties, efficient facilities, and to utilize these together with the colleges for its state-wide needs.

Now one of the most unique aspects of this cunning attempt to capture the University of Wichita was the composition of the board which would develop the new extension center and would report directly to the Board of Regents. On this point Mr. Eurich recommended:

> The University of Kansas and Kansas State University should be authorized to: 1. Establish a State University Center at Wichita under a new board consisting of a. the Chancellor of the University of Kansas (Chairman), b. the President of the Kansas State University (Vice-chairman), c. two academic deans, one each from the University of Kansas and Kansas State University, d. two graduate deans, one each from the University of Kansas and Kansas State University, e. two engineering deans, one each

---

27. Alvin C. Eurich, *et al.*, Kansas: Plans for the Next Generation (Topeka: Board of Regents, 1962), p. 27.

from the University of Kansas and Kansas State University, f. two education deans, one each from the University of Kansas and Kansas State
University, and g. the executive head of the center.[28]

Another interesting recommendation of that report by Mr. Eurich
was that a new Council of State Colleges be formulated with its own
president who would act as chief executive officer of the state college system. This would have meant that the presidents of the three
state colleges at Emporia, Pittsburg, and Fort Hayes would no longer
have reported directly to the Board of Regents.

It is my view that both of these major recommendations illustrate
the interlocking relationship between foundations, former university
presidents who generally head them, and the prestigious universities
which attempt to use the influence, prestige, and consulting services
of the foundations and other voluntary cartels to enhance their own
position of power even at the expense of all other subordinate institutions of higher learning within a given state.

Between 1959 and 1961, I served as director of a study of the
Resources and Needs for Higher Education in Iowa. One of the most
debated recommendations involved the establishment of Comprehensive Regional Community Colleges. To my knowledge, no leaders
from any public or private colleges or universities supported my
recommendation. But four dinner meetings with legislators (about
ninety percent of them) in four different regions of the state convinced me that the people of Iowa were back of the community
college program. The bill was passed, and by 1971 there were 22,000
students in the regional community colleges.

It took Iowa's three major state institutions of higher learning (all
now enjoying university status) over 100 years to grow to 22,000
students.

However, the Establishment does not see the above result as a
blessing but (in the words of one representative, at least) as a curse.
Herbert W. Fort, admissions director at Drake University in Des
Moines noted, in 1971, that much of the squeeze on private schools
resulted from the proliferation of two-year community colleges. He
declared: "We've been very fortunate, but we worry more about
enrollment every year. You spend all this tax money to cut every-

28. *Ibid.*, pp. 9-10.

body's throat, including the state schools, in operating the junior colleges."[29]

I do not believe that the 22,000 students (many of whom could not have gained admission to Drake or the state universities in prosperous times) are getting their throats cut.

THE SINECURE IN AMERICAN SOCIETY

One of the most serious problems of higher education on the continent of Europe for at least a hundred years has been the sinecure. The appointment of an individual to a professorship virtually gave him license to live the life of ease, to enjoy great prestige and comparatively high income, and to follow those scholarly activities associated with his discipline.

The absence of any effective organization or administration of the continental universities and the absence of any effective administrators made it relatively easy for the senicure to follow his own inclinations without regard to the consequences for students, society, or anyone else.

The pattern of the professorship took a different turn in most of the Latin American countries where professors generally are members of some profession outside of the university. They work part time in the university; enjoy status and prestige but receive very little income from the universities. This has been especially true in San Marcos University and in many others throughout Latin America.

During the decade of the sixties, the professorship in the United States took on the characteristics of its counterparts in both Europe and Latin America. Ever since the organization of the AAUP in 1915, professors have become increasingly independent of trustees and administrators because of the commitment of all concerned to academic freedom and tenure and the insistence upon the part of professors that they were not employees of the trustees. They are employed by the trustees, but Supreme Court Justices are appointed by the president and confirmed by the Senate, yet they are not employees of the president.

---

29. *U.S. News and World Report* (September 6, 1971), p. 42.

Academic freedom and tenure combined with responsibility to the society and the university paying the bill are indispensable concomitants of effective scholarly work in any field, however, faculties are not noted for their concern regarding the larger purposes of higher education. I believe they are wise in resisting either a business, military, or governmental approach to organization of the university.

The conservation of useful or valued knowledge and ideas has been a prime responsibility of faculties in all universities. However, this function sometimes is emphasized at the expense of needed change as observed by Mayer.

> Reformers, like President Wayland at Brown, were regarded with suspicion especially when Brown tried to stress modern history and modern languages instead of the classics. The academic scholars were shocked, and for a while regarded the Brown degree as being practically worthless. Scientific studies were slighted at Columbia before 1850. A scientific course which was established in 1830 had to be given up thirteen years later because of lack of student interest. Princeton was so proud of its theological and academic orthodoxy that one theologian rejoiced that not a single new idea had emerged out of Princeton in the fifty years of his professorship.[30]

Faculties have been guilty of pursuing objectives of research and graduate teaching at the expense of undergraduates whom the appropriations of funds were intended to serve. The pattern is a familar one. Funds are allocated that would be sufficient for every undergraduate to be taught by regular faculty members. Most senior professors and many at the assistant level teach only graduate students or do no teaching. The instruction of undergraduates is left to graduate assistants for whom the teaching is a secondary interest compared with pursuit of an advanced degree.

> As Harold Howe II, the U.S. Commissioner of Education, reminded the American Association of University Professors, many professors are so busy consulting and helping run the world outside the campus gates that they have no time for the student or his problems within the gates. The siege of Morningside Heights is one result of that neglect.[31]

Research activities, with little or no coordination or evaluation even within individual universities, are initiated and carried out in terms of the whims of professors thereby siphoning off from undergraduate teaching the most experienced and most expensive

---

30. Frederick Mayer, *Creative Universities* (New York: College and University Press), p. 42.
31. Diamond, *et al., op. cit.,* p. 53.

personnel. No one questions the need for supporting research but the cost should not be extracted from appropriations made for teaching. Even more immoral is the practice of diverting to research tuition and fees collected from undergraduates to support instruction. Sociologist Talcott Parsons has commented on the problem of faculty participation in governance by noting:

> It is my personal view that faculties are not well suited to take the major collective responsibility for a very large part of the corporate affairs of even their own faculties, to say nothing of a university as a whole. . . . At the simpler social level, they are not accountable to anyone but their individual and collective consciences with respect to the guardianship of the integrity of their professional commitments.
>
> It is for other agencies in the society to say how highly these commitments are valued, relative to others, and what resources and protections should be made available to those who have such commitments.[32]

Parsons has also explained why faculties cannot lead political action groups in stating:

> They are not primarily a political group. They do not, and in my opinion should not, have the political decision-making power to decide in their own case, except in what are essentially their internal affairs. Above all, academic faculties and departments should not be subject to pressure to streamline into 'efficient organizations.' In the sense in which canons of efficiency have justified primacy in business firms or governmental administrative organizations, the academic horse is one of a very different color.[33]

Increase in the status of professors and the demand for their services outside of the university have not generally improved education conditions for students.

In the decade of the sixties the professors' being absent from campus contributed to student unrest and general dissatisfaction with the American university of 1971. Disciplines tended to become professionalized. Higher education, in the language of Harold Stoke, became a public utility—meaning something that affects everybody and that everybody wants. Business, industry, agriculture, government, research establishments, church organizations, national and international associations increasingly look to the university for expertise on the part of personnel employed full time and for consulting services in everything from agriculture to space science.

---

32. Talcott Parsons, *The Strange Case of Academic Organizations* (The Journal of Higher Education, June 1971), p. 494.
33. *Ibid.,* p. 495.

Higher education became a public utility because its consequences affect everybody.

The professor as a professional whose discipline became a public utility began to divide his time between the university and his professional activities outside of the university. In hundreds of cases the university was paying less than half of the professor's income.

This professionalization of the disciplines and the resulting part-time professors have made faculty-student ratios absolutely meaningless and we ought to admit this. Although the faculty-student ratio at Harvard may be one to five, many of the undergraduate classes at Harvard are as large as they are in other colleges where the ratio is one to twenty. Perhaps all undergraduate institutions should be staffed at the ratio of one to twenty or twenty-five and then use peer groups or upper classmen as tutors to help those students who have academic problems. Financial implications of such a policy would be astounding in the economies that could be effected, and the educational implications could be equally favorable.

What is called for is a more complete and more intelligent utilization of learning resources other than professors. Libraries, audiovisual materials, television, and the apprenticeship could all be used to supplement the unimaginative things that sometimes go on in the classrooms. The external degree certainly needs a chance to compete with the campus-based degree.

With college and university administrators jetting from one part of the nation and one part of the world to another in order to maintain their responsibilities to the conglomerate cartels and with professors dropping in and out of the university at will in order to man their professional responsibilities to the public utility as well as to pay some slight attention to their academic responsibilities to students, it is high time that members of the Establishment extend similar privileges to students. They should be permitted to drop in and out at will without penalty. A system of evaluation, grading, attendance, and drive to complete the college degree at the magic age of twenty-one or twenty-two should be abandoned. Moreover, the degree itself as a status symbol rather than an educational one should be abandoned.

BUREAUCRACIES AND AUTONOMY

Samuel Gould, former head of the sprawling State University of New York, the largest with which any president has been afflicted thus far, was not at all sanguine about the status of universities in 1970. He observed:

> If we say, and quite appropriately, that the university has never been more necessary and central to our national life than it is today, we must also say that no other major institution in this country is now so open to disbalance and in so precarious a state of health. The university has rarely, if ever, been looked upon by American society with more suspicion, more distrust, or more overt animosity. Many people today seriously question the necessity or the advisability of supporting it. Many more question its structure, policies, programs, achievements, and its capacity for self-discipline and renewal.
>
> If we say that the academic community has made mighty contributions to the progress and reforms of the entire world, we must also add immediately that the university's capacity to change things applies largely off campus and not within its walls.[34]

Professors in highly specialized disciplines and specialized administrators who see the operation from only one narrow viewpoint represent a centrifugal force which, without a counterinfluence applied to an effective organization will bring about the disintegration of any university. Teachers, scholars, and research experts do not want to be overorganized. Oxford University calls itself a collegiate university because the center of power is in the college not in the university. American universities for the most part are departmental universities because the center of power is in the department, which makes our universities a step closer to anarchy than Oxford.

The system gets perpetuated because in keeping with the Peter Principle, noted scholars, with an inherited antipathy towards organization and administration, get elevated to deanships, vice-presidencies and presidencies. Then they become specialists in developing the central bureaucracy. The universal solution to incompetents in administration is growth in personnel. I have known more than one academic man who revealed that his condition for accepting an administrative post was authority to appoint enough assistants to relieve him of all the work and most of the responsibilities.

---

34. Samuel B. Gould, *Today's Academic Condition* (New York: McGraw-Hill Book Co., 1970), p. 7.

Boards of trustees, ostensibly responsible for broad university policy and allocation of resources, have become obsolete in terms of their competence, time, or power to maintain fiscal or personnel prudence in university operations. Although this seems like harsh criticism of individuals who serve on governing boards, it is intended as a frank admission of the growing complexity of universities and the internal bureaucracies that really control them and tend to manipulate governing boards. The truth of the matter is that each major university has become so large that no one knows what goes on, not even the president.

Although the size of an individual university defies understanding or governance, boards of trustees and presidents are reaching out to encircle other universities and colleges to create university systems. Such swallowing up of other far-flung campuses is always in the name of greater educational opportunity, efficiency, economy and organizational and administrative expertise, notwithstanding the fact that each campus has all the administrators it would need without the central bureaucracy.

Autonomy remains a valid principle only for the central university. Freedom for faculties to determine curricula is valid for the central campus but inconsequential for all others. Purposes and programs are designed to enhance the center, and all other campuses (where purposes are prefabricated by outsiders) are relegated to the status of a slave who by Plato's definition is someone whose guiding purposes are dictated by another person.

The arguments for the monolithic state system under a central university are about as valid as the one Russia used for gobbling up of Estonia, Latvia, Lithuania and a host of other satellite states. The attractiveness of concentrated power at the center was paramount in Russia and in university systems. In all cases, political and educational, the satellites have been exploited to enhance the center.

In many cases there are rational foundations for multiple campuses. In other cases the reasons are a consequence of the American predilection for bigness, for power over a possible competitor. Peter Sammartino has noted:

> There is a desire for prestige. After all, an institution has a certain status if it can boast of multiple campuses. Some people are impressed by such a pattern. It has an air of a far-flung empire. There is a desire to assure a

supply of students for the upper years. In this case an institution may establish two-year extensions.[35]

Sammartino also discussed the problem of departmental chairmen as related to multiple campuses. His conclusion indicated much greater concern for the bureaucracy and conformity than for education as he observed,

> The question arises as to which system is better: One chairman to cover all campuses or autonomous chairmen on each campus. After experimenting with both systems, it is my recommendation that the best pattern is for an able, active and competent chairman to oversee all campuses with a deputy on the distant campuses. If this is impossible, then there should be regular meetings of separate chairmen with the understanding that the departments should all be following the same syllabi.[36]

A few years ago, Indiana University followed the pattern of one chairman over many remote departments. I always questioned whether the syllabus for sociology I in Gary should be the same as in Bloomington. I also wondered how autonomy could be so irrelevant for the other campuses. Only the drive for concentration of power at the center could justify imposing the departmental chairman at the parent university as chairman of corresponding departments in all satellite colleges, which were frequently referred to as feeders for the central university.

California was noted for developing the system, and at the beginning of the decade of the sixties and earlier, distinguished organizational and educational leaders were predicting that California was to be the pacesetter for other states. Such evaluations and conclusions generally emanated from would-be chancellors or presidents of future university systems. One is reminded that Robert Hutchins stated at one time that he could count on the fingers of one hand the university presidents capable of thinking about the university in terms of fundamental theory.

The university system brought with it the world's greatest university bureaucracy. The inevitable consequence was for administration to become isolated from university functions; and for the bureaucracy to take on purposes of its own, unrelated to educational functions but, clearly indispensable to survival of the bureaucracy. John

---

35. Peter Sammartino, *Multiple Campuses* (Rutherford, N.J.: Fairleigh Dickinson Press, 1964), pp. 4-5.
36. *Ibid.,* p. 8.

Kenneth Galbraith, writing in the June, 1969 issue of *Harper's* stated:

> The tendency of our time is for organization . . . to develop a life and purpose and truth of its own. This tendency holds for all great bureaucracies, both public and private, and their action is not what serves a larger public interest, their belief does not reflect the reality of life. What is done and what is believed are, first and naturally, what serve the goals of the bureaucracy itself. Action in the organization interest, or in response to the bureaucratic truth, can thus be a formula for public disservice or even public disaster.[37]

Professor Galbraith was describing the military-industrial bureaucracy, in particular, but he was also describing bureaucracy as characteristic of organizations in general, both public and private, in American society.

The university system has tended to shake off all characteristics of a university. The community of scholars and masters, if it ever existed in America, has been eclipsed or replaced by a massive bureaucracy far more involved in the political arena to save itself than in the academic arena to help students. Central administration, headed by a president or chancellor, is cut off from contact with any one campus but exercises excessive power over all campuses in the system. Control becomes increasingly remote and removed from the point at which learning, teaching and research take place. Depersonalization of the university, which brought on many of the student problems of the sixties, is greatly increased by the system. Deans of schools and colleges as well as vice-presidents become so involved in the system that they cease to perform the functions or to provide the leadership in areas for which they were employed.

An administrative assistant to an academic vice-president in one of the satellite institutions in California remarked that he and his colleagues felt so remote from the center of power that there was no motivation to advance an innovative idea.

One California president made it clear to me that millions of dollars could have been deleted from budgets (including the one for his institution) during the years of the late sixties without any loss of education or research effectiveness. If California served as the pacesetter in the sixties, perhaps a significant lesson has been learned that can provide a more rational approach to the decade of the seventies.

Perhaps we shall be safe from the errors of a few presidents and

---

37. John Kenneth Galbraith, *How to Control the Military* (*Harper's* Magazine, June 1969), p. 33.

chancellors who posit the plea for a new centralization of power at the top of the university hierarchy as long as men such as President Gould are free to reason otherwise.

> We live in a time and in a society when few authoritarian decisions can be handed down from one person. Even the leaders of our country make no truly important moves without previously consulting with many of their colleagues as well as with other talented or deeply concerned people wherever they can find them. There is a definite trend toward more flexible, shifting, temporary leadership and decision making, a trend that is leading us to a new concept of how leaders will emerge and be used. I believe that the university must accept the trend as a fact and move swiftly to re-examine and revise its governance arrangements. [38]

John J. Corson has observed the increasing demands made upon universities by consequences of the population explosion, Vietnam, poverty, pollution, and the postindustrial society. He believes that the university has been, and increasingly will be, the institution concerned with the shaping of values. . . . The university can avoid the battles over social issues only by finding the structures and practices within which battles may be fought with words and ideas rather than stones and fists. William M. Roth, a university trustee, has observed:

> The rhetoric of faculty governance betrays the usual cultural lag. Through an intricate structure of senates, assemblies, and committees, it maintains the pretense of a self-governing community of scholars. The inaccurate word is "community," for its members are more concerned with doing their own thing than with the general welfare of the particular society that nourishes them. Traditionally, the professor does not want to be bothered by problems of governance. [39]

Pacesetters gained recognition by trying to change the name as well as the meaning of the university. In some cases a facade bigger than the universe was needed to hide the errors going on within the university. Hence, it was a decade of new names, multiversity, communiversity, metroversity, academy, etc., etc. All of these new connotations represent enclaves of power and bureaucracies.

The university did not originate in America and it may not survive here, but it is very apt to survive everywhere else in the world. And if we ever make a rational retreat from bigness as the objective, the

---

38. Gould, *op. cit.*, p. 85.
39. William M. Roth, *Dilemmas of Leadership* (*Saturday Review,* January 10, 1970).

autonomous university and individual colleges will reappear in America.

Robert Hutchins has predicted that to use the university as an instrument by which we become powerful and wealthy is to guarantee the collapse of a civilization.

I believe that the *pacesetter* of the seventies will be the state *university* that *dismantles* the *system* and restores maximum *autonomy* to each institution. And if the bureaucracy does not take the initiative and help to work out a plan for improvement, I believe that citizens, state legislators and governors will perform the task. This will be a consequence of the fact that legislators already find the system incomprehensible in its complexity, yet they are called upon to appropriate astronomical budgets to support a system they do not understand.

Leaders are needed who can strike a rational balance between tradition and change, between principles and expediencies.

> Never has the need for enlightened leadership been so great. As we compare the ideals of men like Jefferson and Adams with the statements of contemporary leaders in politics, we find a decline of thought and a concern with temporary issues rather than with permanent principles. . . . Both warned against the seductions of militarism, and both were certain that the same standards were to prevail in public as in private morality.[40]

Those commitments are as basic in 1972 as they were in the days of the "founding fathers." Values in our society are changing or, as some would claim, disappearing because our leaders have no benchmarks, no philosophy that can be articulated into practice. Without a philosophy and commitment to values, they are banded about as a balloon which when filled with hot air rises and falls with each gust of wind.

The cultivation of power must be replaced with leadership. Concern for maintaining the education bureaucracies should be replaced by dedication to fundamental interests of society and students. Organization, administrators, faculties and financial resources must become the means for developing student talents and improving society.

---

40. Mayer, *op cit.*, pp. 106-107.

CONCLUSION

Higher education in the United States is a paramount national concern, but our legal machinery for dealing with colleges and universities is provincial. This has brought about the crisis in philosophy or purposes because the federal government has used the power of the treasury to hire universities and professors to engage in research and educational programs initiated by the U.S. Government.

The increasing monopoly of taxes by the federal government has made it virtually impossible for local states to support education. University leaders, in many instances, have resisted the loss of autonomy and freedom inherent in the present situation, but the financial problem has caused fundamental purposes to be compromised.

Universities have capitulated to special interest groups at the national level. Higher education itself has become a special interest group. Moreover, if one examines the budget of the federal government for higher education and its distribution among all the departments and bureaucracies of government, it becomes painfully clear that they are special interest groups.

Students in most countries, and especially in the United States, are protesting the capitulation of universities to values and centers of power that discerning students and citizens cannot accept. These centers of power are military, economic, and political in nature.

At the inauguration of A. Lawrence Lowell as President of Harvard, James Bryce, as one of the speakers, made the following statement: "A university should reflect the spirit of the times, without yielding to it."[41]

Having yielded, I fear that we have lost the function of critic and adjudicator among competing special interests and purposes.

References

1. Bressler, Marvin. "The American College: Some Problems and Choices," *Annals of the American Academy of Political and Social Science*, July 1971.
2. Curti, Merle, and Carstensen, Vernon. *The University of Wisconsin, A History*, Vol. II. University of Wisconsin Press, 1949.

---

41. Merle Curti and Vernon Carstensen, *The University of Wisconsin, A History,* Vol. II (Madison: University of Wisconsin Press, 1949), p. 611.

3. Diamond, Martin, Fisk, Winston M., and Garfinkel, Herbert. *The Democratic Republic: An Introduction to American National Government.* Chicago: Rand McNally and Co., 1966.

4. Dobbins, Charles, and Lee, Calvin B.J. *Whose Goals for American Higher Education?* Washington, D.C.: American Council on Education, 1968.

5. Dye, Thomas R., and Zeigler, Harmon. *Irony of Democracy—Common Introduction to American Politics.* Belmont, California: Duxbury Press, 1971.

6. Eurich, Alvin C., *et al., Kansas: Plans for the Next Generation.* Board of Regents, Topeka, 1962.

7. Galbraith, John Kenneth. "How to Control the Military," *Harper's Magazine,* June 1969.

8. Gould, Samuel B. *Today's Academic Concition.* New York: McGraw-Hill Book Company, 1970.

9. International Association of Universities, Bulletin: Vol. XVIII, No. 4, Paris, 1970.

10. Mayer, Frederick. *Creative Universities.* New York: College and University Press, 1961.

11. Michels, Robert. *Political Parties: A Sociological Study of the Oligarchical Tendencies of Modern Democracy.* Translated by Eden and Cedar Paul. Glencoe, Illinois: The Free Press, 1966.

12. Parsons, Talcott. "The Strange Case of Academic Organizations," *Journal of Higher Education,* June 1971.

13. Roth, William M. "Dilemmas of Leadership," *Saturday Review.* January 10, 1970.

14. Sandburg, Carl. *Abraham Lincoln, The Prairie Years.* New York: Harcourt, Brace and Co., 1927.

15. Searle, John R. *The Campus War.* New York: The World Publishing Co., 1971.

16. Seidenbaum, Art. *Confrontation on Campus.* Los Angeles: The Ward Ritchie Press, 1969.

17. Stedman, Murray S., Jr., (ed.). *Modernizing American Government.* Englewood Cliffs, N.J.: Prentice-Hall, Inc., 1968.

18. Schattschneider, E.E. *The Semisovereign People; A Realist's View of Democracy in America.* New York: Holt Rinehart & Winston, Inc., 1960.

19. Sammartino, Peter. *Multiple Campuses.* Rutherford, N.J.: Fairleigh Dickinson University Press, 1964.

20. *U.S. News and World Report.* September 6, 1971.

21. Wolff, Robert Paul. *The Ideal of the University.* Boston: Beacon Press, 1969.

2

The University Grants Committee of Great Britain Prototype for Block Grants

I will not conceal my belief that this (the U.G.C.) is one of the happiest of our constitutional inventions. Whatever may be its role in the future, it would be difficult to deny that, so far, it has operated in such a way as to permit the transmission to the universities of an ever-increasing volume of public money without serious encroachment on academic freedom.

Lord Robbins

Following the First World War, the British Government began to provide much greater support for the universities. The University Grants Committee was organized in 1919. It included seventeen members with the chairman working full time. Two other members sat with the committee when academic salaries were being considered. Members of the committee (serving five-year terms) and an executive secretary were appointed by the Chancellor of the Exchequer with the approval of the Prime Minister.

There was no official connection with the Ministry of Education, although it became a custom for a representative of the Ministry of Education to attend meetings of the committee in order to maintain desirable liaison between different levels of education.

U.G.C. was responsible only for the universities. Colleges of advanced technology, teacher's colleges and other nondegree granting institutions presented their budgetary requests to the Ministry of Education.

The members of the U.G.C., other than the chairman and the executive secretary, are honorary workers. They come from academic staffs of universities, from the professions and industry, and some are directors of local education units. The object in making the selection is to have all important branches of knowledge and of British society represented. Vice-chancellors of the universities are not appointed to the committee. They appear before the committee to present budgetary requests and to consider national policy for higher education.

Grants are made to the universities on a quinquennial (five-year) basis. The grant made to each university takes the form of a block grant to be used at the discretion of the university over the entire range of its activities. Since the Second World War, there have been earmarked grants for medicine, dentistry, agriculture, veterinary sciences, and social studies; Oriental, African, and Slavic studies; and science and technology. It is generally anticipated that earmarked grants, initiated by the government or by the universities, will shortly become a part of block grants on a recurring quinquennial basis.

The frame of reference of U.G.C. as announced by the Chancellor of the Exchequer in 1946 was to assist, in consultation with universities and other bodies concerned, in the preparation and execution of such plans for the development of universities as may from time to time be required in order to ensure that they are fully adequate to national needs. The British Government regards the universities as indispensable to the cultural, economic, and political life of the nation. This policy demands coordinated planning involving universities, government, and national needs unknown in British universities of the past.

It is generally conceded that independence and autonomy for the universities, as the system has developed, contributed effectively to the national interest.

The executive secretary of U.G.C. has stated the policy clearly, noting that the government called upon the universities to meet certain manpower requirements in science and technology, and that the government provided the necessary financial resources for achieving the objective. Responses of the universities to requests, adequately supported by the government, have been satisfactory in every way. The cooperation has been unique.[1]

METHODS OF OPERATION[2]

U.G.C. has the policy of visiting each university beginning about the middle of the quinquennium. The objective is to have at least one-half of the committee visit each university. It took 108 days to

---

1. Raymond C. Gibson, *The Challenge of Leadership in Higher Education* (Dubuque, Iowa: Wm. C. Brown Company Publishers, 1964), pp. 325-27.
2. *Ibid.*, pp. 327-28.

carry out this task in preparation for the 1962-67 quinquennial budget. These visits provide members with first-hand information on which they can determine fiscal policy.

By the end of the fourth year of each quinquennium, all requests, with supporting tables, statistics, and relevant data, are submitted to U.G.C. by the various universities. These requests include new programs as well as recurring operations. Vice-chancellors appear before the committee to explain and justify their requests.

The requests take the form of a total grant for the universities. Generally, in March preceding the end of the quinquennium, which is July 31, the government announces the grants for the five-year period beginning the first of August. Following this announcement, U.G.C. has the responsibility of making an equitable distribution of the total funds among the institutions involved.

The University Grants Committee serves in an intermediary position between the national government and the universities. The universities have no direct contact with the Treasury or Ministry of Education and are spared the undesirable task of competing with one another and with other agencies of government in the political arena.

Within the limitations imposed by the amount of grant to a university, there is internal freedom for the faculty and administration to proceed with their own plans for the next quinquennium. The exception to this would be in the case of funds earmarked by government or by the universities in their original requests; e.g., if a university requests funds for a specific new function and receives the funds, it would be obligated to carry out that responsibility.

Following the completion of the quinquennial grants, the secretariat is free to devote its time to various problems confronting higher education. For example, U.G.C., in cooperation with the vice-chancellors, sponsored studies that eventuated in a recommendation to the government that new universities be established. This reflects an intelligent response to the demand for expansion of higher education.

When U.G.C. was established in 1919, the budget for higher education was only a fraction of what it has been in recent years. As late as 1939, the year the second great war started, funds granted to the universities amounted to only $5,300,000. By 1961-62, grants amounted to $210,000,000, and provided about seventy percent of the operating budgets and ninety-five percent of the building programs of British universities. The enormous increase during the 1939-62 period was considerably out of proportion to the increase in student population, which grew from 50,000 in 1938-39 to approximately 111,000 in 1961-62. In twenty-two years, the enrollment increased by approximately 122 percent, but the contribution of the British Government increased by 3,862 percent.

In the year 1967-68 the universities received £216.6 million, chiefly as a recurrent grant from the Exchequer. Full-time students at British universities totaled 211,485 in 1967-68. The ratio of students to staff has tended to be stable at 8:1 since 1958.[3]

Beginning in the fall of 1962, every university student in Great Britain received government support for at least a part of the expense of his education. Even the son of a wealthy family received £50, after which the "means test" was applied. Capable students from very poor families received complete support for their university education. Britain has rejected the idea of loans instead of grants for needy students. One cannot help admiring this inclination to pay for higher education out of current income instead of passing the burden on to another generation, with interest and administrative costs added.[4]

More than ninety percent of all home students at British universities receive awards paying part or all of their fees and other expenses. "Undergraduate students in higher education who do not receive public support are mainly students in further education who receive assistance from their employers. Despite periodic pressure to replace the grant system with loans, such a change appears unlikely."[5]

The British made significant changes in the system as a result of the Robbins Committee Report in 1963, but the principal elements of the system have been validated by experience. There is no inclination to abandon the most successful aspects of the scheme. Note this statement from the President of the Association of University Teachers made in 1964.

> I suppose that behind all our discussions will be the ever-present problem that universities face, and that is the striking of a balance between the

---

3. *International Association of Universities* (Paris: Vol. XVIII, No. 4, 1970), p. 259.
4. Gibson, *op. cit.,* p. 329.
5. Barbara B. Burn, Philip G. Altbach, Clark Kerr, and James A Perkins, *Higher Education in Nine Countries* (New York: McGraw-Hill Book Company, 1971), p. 77.

university's freedom to develop its academic programme and the quite legitimate demand of government to have some control over the spending of the money which they provide. This is a problem which different countries have met in different ways, but I think we should all agree that the British contribution to this problem is a major one, and although we may see some aspects in which our system could be developed, in the main we should view with alarm any suggestion that there should be major changes in the system which we have developed over the years.[6]

On the problem of capital grants, Dr. Chattaway emphasized the importance of long-range planning when he said, "It is important to realize that we want not simply a quinquennial capital programme but one that . . . remains valid five years ahead by being reviewed annually."[7]

There is general agreement that the only way that adequate research and study can be brought to bear upon the allocation of operating and capital funds is to use a period of four or five years as the minimum planning period.

A noted British leader, Eric Ashby has stated the case for the status of universities as a world development. His view also explains why Commonwealth countries have considerable similarity in their approach to higher education:

> The balance sheet for British colonialism includes four substantial assets: Christianity, representative government, educational institutions and the English language. Of these four assets the most universally acceptable, and the least changed by the indigenous cultural environment, are the educational institutions exported from Britain to her Commonwealth.
>
> The export of higher education from Britain began over three hundred years ago when John Harvard, from Emmanuel College, Cambridge, left his property to the college just opened in Massachusetts, and Henry Dunster, from Magdalene College, Cambridge, was appointed president of the college.[8]

BRITISH AND AMERICAN EVALUATION

Sir Douglas Logan, Principal of the University of London, considers that the root of much trouble for British universities is their excessive financial dependence on the State, and says that things will get worse unless the trend is reversed. Universities have to argue with the University Grants Committee, the Committee has to argue with the Department of Educa-

---

6. T.W. Chattaway, *The Financing of Universities.* Home Universities Conference (London: The Association of Commonwealth Universities, 1964), p. 48.
7. *Ibid.,* p. 49.
8. Eric Ashby, *Community of Universities: An Informal Portrait of the Association of the Universities of the British Commonwealth* (Cambridge: The University Press, 1900), pp. 92-93.

tion and Science and the department has to argue with the Treasury. This procedure is time-wasting in the extreme.[9]

Sir Douglas would reform the system of support by shifting fifty percent of the costs to students. He made three specific recommendations on this problem.

1. Half of expenditure of universities should be met by Treasure block grants.
2. The balance of the expenditure of universities should be met by raising tuition fees to something approaching North American levels, *viz.* £500–£600.
3. The present system of student awards, with its involvement in the perennial conflict of central and local authority finance, should be scrapped and with it the parental contribution. In its place, there should be substituted arrangements under which a student, if he wishes, can obtain grants to cover his maintenance and tuition fees on condition that he accepts an obligation during his working life to have a small percentage of his earned income deducted at source, in the same way as income tax.[10]

Barbara Burn, Kerr, *et al.,* believe that other problems will become increasingly serious for U.G.C. in the future. They stated:

A major problem in the future appears to be the determination of criteria for allocating funds and supporting expansion in the two sectors of British higher education. . . . The universities are sometimes criticized for not being sufficiently responsive to the needs of society. This criticism raises the basic philosophical problem of whether the university itself can best evaluate and decide how to serve society most effectively or whether society should determine what needs the university meets, and how. This problem may be more acute in Britain than in North American universities because the chief executive officer in British universities has relatively less authority. The major role of faculty members in university governance, carried to the ultimate at Oxford and Cambridge, militates against strong central direction by the organ of governance best suited to look equally within and without the immediate academic community.[11]

This evaluation is typical of our American proclivity for centralization of authority in a chief executive—whether the institution be government, industry, the army, or (of all things) a university. How could one conclude that a major problem in Britain (rather than in the United States) will be the determination of criteria for allocating funds? If the British changed to our system of earmarking every dollar for a purpose determined by the government, this certainly would be a problem.

9. *International Association of Universities* (Paris: Vol. XIV, No. 3, 1966), p. 174.
10. *Ibid.,* p. 174.
11. Barbara B. Burn, *et al., op. cit.,* pp. 84-85.

Moreover, I prefer the collective intelligence of faculties, senates and the university council (including academic and lay members) to the "lengthened shadow" concept implied in "strong central direction."

On these and other points, I also believe the chairman of U.G.C., Mr. Wolfenden, has spoken from a background of experience that tends to refute the American view of the U.G.C. system.

> I have deliberately spoken of the balance between teaching and research rather than of a conflict between them. And I dogmatically assert that the keeping of this balance is the responsibility of the faculty—or what we call the academic staff. Under our British system, the recurrent grant which is made to a university is a block grant for each of the five years ahead. A university's application to the University Grants Committee is itemized in great detail, and the details are very carefully scrutinized. But at the end of the day, the allocation of public funds to the university is, with very rare exceptions in very special circumstances, a block sum, without strings. Decisions on how these funds are to be deployed inside the university rest solely with the university itself, including the decision on how much money is to be spent on teaching and how much on research. . . . When I say "the university," I may well seem, to American ears, to fall short of proper precision. But, with all due respect, that is exactly what I mean. Recommendations about such decisions as these are made by the university senate, usually on the initiative of the heads of the various departments. Before a proposal gets to the senate, it has been exhaustively, and exhaustingly, discussed at departmental meetings, faculty boards, and senate committees. . . . Eventually, there is a senate decision based on genuinely (I was going to say "purely") academic grounds.[12]

It appears to me that the council, as described by Wolfenden would be an appropriate alternative to the usual board of regents in the United States which generally excludes academics and relies exclusively upon one central administrator to speak for the total university. A rational mix of lay and faculty members would keep the educational consequences of budgetary decisions on a par with bureaucratic concerns. On this process, Wolfenden has noted:

> Now comes an important point. This academic decision goes forward to the university council, the continuing body which is ultimately responsible for the university's financial affairs. This body has a majority of nonacademics: businessmen, industrialists, lawyers, whatever—and a substantial minority of members of that same senate who sit on precisely equal terms with those whom we affectionately call the "lay" members. In my experience of trying to run a university, I never encountered a division on my council between the academics on the one hand and the nonacademics on

---

12. Dobbins and Lee, *op. cit.*, pp. 210-11.

the other. And I have never known a senate recommendation on an academic matter to be rejected by the council except for the simple reason that there was no money for it.

Mercifully, university senates and councils are not composed of introverted, self-regarding half-wits. They recognize that, whereas universities in Britain were once small private corporations existing on fees and the endowments of pious benefactors, they are now intimately enmeshed in a society which financially supports them, and, at the same time, tolerates a remarkable degree of autonomy for each institution.[13]

The last paragraphs above certainly need to be considered by governors and other officials who make appointments to coordinating and governing boards for higher education in the United States.

On all sides, university people argued that eternal vigilance was necessary: yet none could cite evidences of overt direction or interference with university policy or, indeed, with the independence of the universities. Some persons—laymen, largely—deplored the hands-off policy of the U.G.C. . . . In a sense, this was a demand for more intervention. But of the reverse, of evidences of undue meddling, there was none.[14]

Hacker stated that the Chancellor of the Exchequer, the U.G.C., the Minister of Education and the Department of Scientific and Industrial Research were committed to upholding the independence of the universities.

Lindsey Rogers, writing on the U.G.C., wondered whether the system would work in the U.S. He concluded that should Congress make a blanket grant to any department of the U.S. Government for higher education, its head and his civil servants would use the authority to divide up the money. They would do it themselves or establish a new bureau to do it.[15]

Profiteering in new activities and in new personnel might cost something in criticism of specific decisions, but this would not seem too high a price to pay for the exercise of power. Indeed, President Truman vetoed the Congressional plan to have a National Science Foundation directed by a nonpolitical board which would be relatively free from the statutory limitations on administrative discretion that Congress so often insists on imposing. Important policies and large expenditures, the President declared, would be determined by individuals who are 'essential private citizens' whom he could not hold effectively responsible.[16]

---

13. *Ibid.*, pp. 211-13.
14. Harold W. Dodds, Louis M. Hacker and Lindsay Rogers, *Government Assistance to Universities in Great Britain* (New York: Columbia University Press, 1952), p. 62.
15. *Ibid.*, p. 80.
16. *Ibid.*, p. 80.

Harold W. Dodds was not so generous toward the U.G.C. He concluded:

> Nevertheless, the universities are not free in the sense of the self-determination they enjoyed twenty-five years ago. True, they have not been nationalized after the pattern of the railways and steel industry.
>
> U.G.C. is the resultant of a complex of circumstances, traditions, and governmental practices peculiar to Great Britain. Like the British Constitution, it is not exportable. The peculiar features which have made the system uniquely successful, as against what obtains in other countries, are not to be discovered in statutory law or administrative arrangements which could be copied in the U.S. with the expectation that they would function with us as they do in Britain. For they are the fruit of a social complex of attitudes, conventions, and, most significantly, personal relations which are foreign to us and contrary to our governmental practices and political mores.[17]

Mr. Dodds admitted that the system was uniquely successful but could not be exported. Twenty years after his conclusion was written, the U.G.C. system had been exported to Canada, Australia, New Zealand, Hong Kong, India and Pakistan. I submit that India, Canada, and Australia are more similar to the U.S. than to Great Britain. They have state systems of education, and each is geographically near the size of the U.S.

All English speaking countries tend to prove that principles of parliamentary government may be exported successfully.

Mr. Dodds admitted that the time had passed when a university could hope to operate on the basis of its own estimate of the concerns of the nation and how best to serve them. One has to raise the question of whether the self-determination of Princeton University, of which Mr. Dodds was president at the time of his research on U.G.C., has fared better under our federal system of categorical grants than it would have under a system more like the U.G.C.

I think that President Truman gave the rationale for direct government control of grants and the functions which they serve. Power is the motive. Political power is more attractive to American politicians, both in government and in the universities, than university autonomy. And, to paraphrase Aristotle, those who crave to exercise power over the universities are generally unqualified to do so, and those competent to exercise control of the universities would not want to do so.

---

17. *Ibid.,* p. 99.

Knowledge and the expertise required for prudent and intelligent exercise of political power, on the part of leaders in government, are dependent upon freedom of research, learning and teaching in the universities. For universities to invade the political arena and politicians overtly to enter into university governance would guarantee the failure of both the state and the university. In 1930, Flexner described the U.G.C. by noting:

> This committee, headed since its inception in 1919 by Sir William S. McCormick, a Scot, who knew at first hand the universities of Scotland, England, Germany, and the United States, has been a gentle, but powerful influence for good. In the absence of control by an education ministry, it has assisted what is good and quietly ignored all else. Its counsel and its funds have been almost equally acceptable.[18]

RATIONALE FOR THE SUCCESS OF THE UNIVERSITY GRANTS SYSTEM[19]

Officials in the British Government, in the Ministry of Education, and in the universities have provided insight into the formal procedures by which U.G.C. operates and the reasons for the success which the scheme has enjoyed since it was first established. There seemed to be agreement among the various segments of the society concerning the desirability of supporting the universities without interfering with their initiative to run their own affairs. Several specific characteristics of the British Government, the universities, and the British people in general have contributed significantly to the success of the University Grants System.

The People Know One Another

Traditions within the government and within the universities have tended to work to the advantage of the University Grants System. Moreover, the fact that appointments to the committee are made for a five-year term and that a majority of the members of the committee come from the colleges and universities, has contributed to the development of a situation which operates as though it were a small village. Many of the leaders in government and in the universities were friends as undergraduate students. Although various members of the Grants Committee are known to their peers among uni-

---

18. Abraham Flexner, *Universities: American, English, German* (New York: Oxford University Press, 1930), p. 251.
19. Gibson, *op. cit.,* pp. 329-33.

versity professors and administrators, there is no evidence that any member of the committee uses his position to represent in a partisan way his own university. Each member represents his area of expertise and the interests of all universities, as every member of a governing or coordinating body should.

Individuals within government, education, the Ministry of Education, and leaders in British society not only know one another but also share a common interest in maintaining their universities at a high standard. University and government officials have learned to trust one another. People in local governments trust the national government, and vice versa. People in the Ministry of Education speak highly of the members of the U.G.C., and of the leaders in the universities. Officials of the universities and in the U.G.C., have confidence in one another and in the government. There is no evidence of a sharp cleavage between local and national governments. Officials in the universities, in the Grants Committee, and in the Ministry of Education regard their positions as a great public trust, designed to preserve freedom in the universities and to keep them cushioned against political influence.

The National Government Enjoys Prestige

It has never occurred to any Englishman that local government could be better than national government. Why should it be? Any student of public administration knows that no one level of government (local, state, or national) has a monopoly on virtue in any nation. This being the case, it has not occurred to university officials or to leaders in British society generally that universities are threatened by drawing most of their financial support from the British Treasury instead of from local units of government. National control could become more of an issue as the treasury grants for higher education increase, but up to now, the universities have enjoyed maximum autonomy. This great precedent, the British government supporting enterprises that it does not control, is a mark of mature government concerned with preserving freedom. The source of support is not the issue. It is whether or not political leaders can resist the temptation to control everything that they support, albeit with the people's own money.

The Civil Service System

The tradition of the British in permitting employees to advance in terms of competencies and personal growth, rather than in terms of the size of bureaucracy which is developed and supervised, has set a precedent for the U.G.C. voluntarily to limit the control which it exercises over the universities. The executive secretary and the chairman of the U.G.C. regard themselves and their organization as an important service agency for the universities in securing government support, by representing the universities to the government, by serving as catalysts to bring about greater interaction between the universities and British society, and by serving as a buffer between the support and control of British universities.

The size of the secretariat and the size of the budget for the U.G.C. are clearly indicative of the absence of bureaucratic tendencies on the part of this organization. Indeed, one of the principal criticisms of those who would seriously change the U.G.C. is that the central office in London is inadequately staffed and that perhaps there are not enough members on the committee to cope with the increasing size and complexity of the program of higher education. The budget for the U.G.C's central office in London is less than one percent of the grants secured for the universities. This percentage is probably below the cost of raising funds, either from government or from private sources, in any college or university, public or private, in the United States or in any other country.

The Depreciation of Power

One of the most unique aspects of the British Government and British universities is the fact that status is not synonymous with power. The civil servant, who is inducted into the government at an early age on the basis of his ability to do a specific task and to grow in stature as a government servant, as well as the vice-chancellor, the dean, or the professor in a university, do not gain status in terms of the number of people whom they supervise. The drive, therefore, to build up large bureaucracies and to control large groups of people as a method of gaining status, so characteristic of other governments, has not become a characteristic of British Government in general, or of the universities. The professor gets his status on the basis of competence in his field of specialization. Even if he becomes Master of a House at Cambridge, or if he becomes Vice-chancellor of the University, these positions do not carry tremendous power. It is believed that the absence of power as an index of status in government and in the universities has been a psychological factor in limiting the authority of the government over the universities. When there is no tangible reward for the possession of power, it becomes less attractive to officials in government and in education.

Most of the key officials of the British Government are graduates of universities. They do not hesitate to defend the integrity and the freedom of universities to pursue their objectives without interference from government officials.

Party Discipline

Political parties in Britain are far less susceptible to special interest groups than in the United States. Party discipline is greater and the influence of lobbyists is far less as a consequence.

STATUS OF U.G.C. IN 1970

The University Grants Committee now has twenty-two members. Most of the members are professors from the various universities. One is the chief education officer from a county council. A few are prominent laymen. The chairman was formerly the bursar at King's College, Cambridge University, and a special economic adviser to the British Treasury.

Since the implementation of the Robbins Committee Report, which came out in 1963, members of the committee have been appointed by the Secretary of State for Education and Science. Individuals are nominated by the vice-chancellor's committee, by U.G.C. itself, and by the Department of Education and Science. However, the final invitations to serve on the committee are extended by the Secretary of State for Education and Science.

The above description of the process by which the committee is appointed indicates the change in the chain of command brought about by the Robbins Committee Report.

Another important change was within the Ministry of Education itself. At the head of the department is the Secretary of State for Education and Science. Under that office there are three Ministers of State: one for Arts, one for Universities and Further Education, and one for the Schools. In addition, there is a Parliamentary Under-secretary of State for Education which is a staff position, and there are two permanent Undersecretaries and one Deputy Undersecretary of State for Education. Finally, there is a Secretary for Welsh Education, this being a permanent civil service position, and the individual in this position may report directly to the Secretary of State for Education.

The chain of command for the presentation of university requests is as follows: vice-chancellors present their requests directly to U.G.C. which submits quinquennial recurrent and nonrecurrent requests to the Department of Education which in turn submits its requests to the Treasury.

Thus, the vice-chancellors deal with U.G.C. as they did prior to the reorganization. Moreover, the Department of Education relies upon the supporting research and data provided by U.G.C. instead of going out to do its own research to determine the quinquennial grants. The Department of Education may reduce or augment the quinquennial request submitted by U.G.C.

Still another significant change initiated in 1964 was authority for the Government Accounts Committee regularly to audit the books of the universities. The universities had enjoyed a kind of immunity to the Accounts Committee in previous years, and members of Parliament (generally graduates of the universities) had defended this fiscal autonomy as necessary and desirable for the universities.

In discussing with bursars in the universities their specific relationships with government auditors, I found no resentment toward the process by which the auditors were operating, and, indeed, there was an indication of positive advantage to the universities in providing accountability for the expenditure of public funds and in receiving government sanction that prudent fiscal policy did obtain in the universities.

The Secretary of U.G.C. indicated that placing the organization under the Secretary of State for Education, and more directly under the Minister of State for Universities and Further Education, opened the way for coordination of education at all levels and gave the universities a chance to be more sensitive to the schools of the country.

There is evidence that all officials recognize the need for greater articulation within the total school system including the universities.

For example, on the first of May 1970, the Secretary of State for Education, who was being given a bad time over his support of the comprehensive high school idea, stated in the House of Commons "the eleven-plus examination is the greatest inequity in British education—the last great social barrier." It should be noted that the eleven-plus examination determines at that age whether a student may pursue secondary education leading to university entrance or be relegated to a more practical curriculum leading to employment.

The most important result of the reorganization was that it left the universities under the U.G.C. Vice-chancellors deal with U.G.C. and not with the Department of Education. U.G.C. continues to serve as a buffer between the universities and the political arena.

Another important result indicated by the executive secretary was that budgetary requests submitted by U.G.C. may be trimmed or augmented by the Department of Education. He indicated also that the recurring block grant is a fixed amount which is not subject to change except to meet increased costs each year. This provides flexibility to meet changes in crises including salary changes.

The secretary indicated that the amalgamation of some technological colleges into the university system was highly justified in most cases but that separation may be just as valid where enrollments are large enough that nothing is gained by way of efficiency and economy by bringing the two types of institutions together. It was felt that this problem needs further study before any long-range policy can be determined.

Teacher education is another aspect of higher education that needs to be studied as part of a larger picture. This aspect of higher education has not yet been given degree status and there is not yet a final conclusion that this is desirable in Britain. On the problem and status of teacher education, Lord Robbins noted in a discussion of his report:

> One of the most significant experiences that I had in the many foreign travels that we made was a visit to the Pedagogic Institute of Leningrad. We had visited the University of Leningrad . . . and the Polytechnic, an institution of equal fame. But after such visits, to go on to the Pedagogic Institute and to see there these fine upstanding men and women stalking about, absolutely confident that they were doing one of the most important jobs in the Soviet Union and not in the least depressed that they were in contact with university people, was a peculiarly striking and significant experience. I remembered the atmosphere that I had found in training colleges at home, where the admirable teachers . . . seemed to be anxious

to convince us that they had some right to live and to academic respect.[20]

The Robbins Committee recommended a transfer of responsibility for the training colleges from local education authorities to the universities, subject to approval by the universities; and that institutes of education become schools of the universities with authority for granting university degrees to those "suited to courses of that standard."

As indicated earlier, the debate on these recommendations was continuing seven years later, but placing all of tertiary education under the Secretary of State for Education and Science may lead to a solution of this problem.

I have noticed that university education for the elite has tended to exclude teacher education (a concern for education for the masses) from degree status in Europe, Asia, and Latin America.

Finally, the executive secretary of U.G.C. pointed out that perhaps the principal reason for bringing the universities under the Department of Education was the fact that most of higher education was already there. Engineering colleges, teachers' colleges and other tertiary education institutions enrolled more students than the universities, and they were under the Department of Education before the reorganization.

In 1970 there were approximately 100 professional staff and personnel working in the London headquarters of the U.G.C. In addition, was there a small civil service staff in the Ministry of State for Universities and Further Education, which maintains close liaison with U.G.C.

REACTIONS OF SELECTED VICE-CHANCELLORS

The following views do not represent a cross section of reactions from vice-chancellors because it was possible to interview only a limited number from a total of forty-five universities.

In general, officials within the universities including vice-chancellors with whom I discussed the new organization indicated that placing U.G.C. under the Department of Education has tended to place certain limitations on the universities.

---

20. Conference of the Universities of the United Kingdom, Report of Proceedings, 1963, pp. 22-23.

One significant change is the fact that the Department of Education makes some rather important decisions regarding substantiative departments and faculties. For example, it may recommend that a university have a faculty of forestry or of agriculture, or it may recommend the closing of such a department or faculty. It should be noted that the Minister of State for Universities does not command the closing of a department—but it is possible to cut off grants for departments in question and leave it to the university to continue the program if it can get the funds.

The Department of Education has imposed building standards and limitations on building costs to the point that it is difficult to get a good building under U.G.C. unless the university digs up supplementary funds. The U.G.C. Manual on Procedure for Nonrecurrent Grants published in 1970 includes fifty-six pages of instructions and procedures to be followed in the procurement of land, new buildings and equipment. The manual is very complete and is an excellent document for guarding the public interest in making certain that buildings are justified, adequately planned and designed to serve the functions for which they were intended. But the procedures are so detailed that serious delays in the completion of buildings are inevitable.

The Accounts Committee, as indicated earlier, now checks to see if funds have been wisely and prudently used. They really go around and raise hell in some cases concerning the misuse of funds on buildings that may be too elaborate. The building of Warwick University is an excellent example of a case where the Accounts Committee, the Minister of State for Universities, and the U.G.C. really needed to scrutinize more carefully the methods by which decisions were made regarding university buildings, their function, their location, and their costs.[21]

It is not unusual under the present scheme for vice-chancellors to be called before the House of Commons to justify all kinds of decisions regarding their universities. Perhaps this is a constructive way of making the universities more sensitive to national needs. Moreover, it may be less painful to appear before the House of Commons than to be visited by a Royal Commission. Those univer-

---

21. E.P. Thompson, *Warwick University Ltd.* (Middlesex: Penguin Books Inc., 1970), pp. 79-81.

sities that have Royal Charters have been shaken up a few times by Royal visits, very much in the public interest.

U.G.C. has assumed more power over the universities as a result of the new scheme but is generally thought to be understaffed to exercise this closer scrutiny of university activities. I personally know of nothing more encouraging than the reluctance on the part of an agency such as U.G.C. to proliferate its bureaucracy in terms of personnel and budget.

There were some arguments for having the U.G.C. functions taken over by the Department of Education which, it was assumed, would be more adequately staffed for performing the functions now divided between U.G.C. and the Department of Education. However, the merit of the buffer-type U.G.C. has very strong support in universities and in the government.

There was consensus among those interviewed in the Department of Education, U.G.C. and in the universities that coordination and the limitation of duplicating programs are legitimate functions of U.G.C., notwithstanding the fact that these actions tend to worry university faculties and administrators. In this drive for excellence combined with fiscal prudence, one is reminded of Flexner's observation that "British university leaders do not believe they will ever indulge in the capers that have made American universities ridiculous; they have too much sense and too little money." J. Stuart Maclure has articulated the central idea of the U.G.C. in stating:

> We therefore lay great emphasis on the principle of control through general block grants administered by an independent committee or commission appointed for its expert qualities, not for its political affiliations. We regard this principle, exemplified in the present system of the University Grants Committee, as one of the significant administrative inventions of modern times: and we attach great importance to its retention and development in the machinery of government of the future.[22]

---

22. J. Stuart Maclure, *Education Documents, England and Wales,* 1818-1967 (London: Chapman and Hall, Ltd., 2nd ed., 1968), p. 295.

References

1. Ashby, Eric. *Community of Universities: An Informal Portrait of the Association of Universities of the British Commonwealth.* Cambridge: University Press, 1963.
2. Burn, Barbara B. *et al. Higher Education in Nine Countries.* New York: McGraw-Hill Book Co., 1971.
3. Chattaway, T.W. *The Financing of Universities: Home Universities Conference.* The Association of Commonwealth Universities, London, 1964.
4. Conference of the Universities of the United Kingdom: Report of Proceedings, London, 1963.
5. Dobbins, Charles G., and Lee, Calvin B.T. *Whose Goals for American Higher Education?* American Council on Education, Washington, D.C., 1968.
6. Dodds, Harold W. *et al. Government Assistance to Universities in Great Britain.* New York: Columbia University Press, 1952.
7. Flexner, Abraham. *Universities: American, English, German.* New York: Oxford University Press, 1930.
8. Gibson, Raymond C. *The Challenge of Leadership in Higher Education.* Dubuque, Iowa: Wm. C. Brown Company Publishers, 1964.
9. International Association of Universities: Bulletin. Vol. XVIII, No. 4, Paris, 1970 and Vol. XIV, No. 3, 1966.
10. Maclure, J. Stuart. *Education Documents, England and Wales, 1816-1967.* London: Chapman and Hall, Ltd., 2nd ed., 1968.
11. Robbins Committee. Higher Education: Report of the Committee Appointed by the Prime Minister under the Chairmanship of Lord Robbins 1961-63. Her Majesty's Stationery Office, London, 1963.
12. Thompson, E.P. Warwick University, Ltd. Middlesex: Penguin Books, Inc., 1970.
13. University Grants Committee. University Development, 1962-67. London: HMSO, 1968.

3

International Principles Applied
to Provincial Problems

The universities of Hong Kong, New Zealand and India are not internationally famous centers of higher learning. They tend to be local universities. In general, they serve local needs. However, political and university leaders have recognized higher education as a national concern. Moreover, they have refused to be provincial in searching for a viable relationship between government and higher education. They have gone beyond national or colonial boundaries in search of principles of organization and financial support of universities.

U.G.C. APPLIED TO THE COLONY OF HONG KONG

In January 1960, the Government of Hong Kong invited Sir Edward Hale (Secretary of U.G.C. in England from 1951-57) to advise the Hong Kong Government on whether a committee, similar to the U.G.C. in Great Britain, should be established to advise the government on the financial needs of the universities in Hong Kong and to allocate to them the financial resources made available by the government towards meeting those needs. Although established in 1965, U.G.C. became operational for the academic year of 1967 on a triennial basis. At the end of the first triennium in June 1970, the recurrent program was changed to a four-year plan, which had been adopted for capital grants from the beginning. In his report to His Excellency, the Governor, entitled *The Financing of Universities in Hong Kong,* Sir Edward said:

> Any government which is financing more than one university has problems to face which can hardly be solved satisfactorily unless it can satisfy public opinion that its action is based on advice from an impartial and expert body, and I feel no doubt that the Hong Kong Government is in need of such a body.[1]

1. *University Grants Committee of Hong Kong* (Hong Kong: At the Government Press by S. Young, Government Printer, December, 1968), p. 3.

Composition of the University Grants Committee

U.G.C. in Hong Kong is composed of ten members, appointed by the governor of the colony. Three members are from Hong Kong, one of these being the chairman, one is from Australia, and six are from England. The chairman and one other Hong Kong member are business executives and a third one from Hong Kong is an attorney. The Australian member is a professor of chemistry at the University of Western Australia. Of the six members from England, four are professors in medicine, English, geography and the arts. One is principal of the Chelsea College of Science and Technology. The sixth member is Deputy Secretary of the U.G.C. in England. These members were initially appointed for a term of five years.

The institutions over which U.G.C. exercises influence are the University of Hong Kong, the New Asia College, Chung Chi College and the United College located in Kowloon which is a part of the mainland of China. U.G.C. is charged with the responsibility of combining the three colleges into one university which will be known as the Chinese University of Hong Kong. The two colleges were scheduled to move to the same campus by 1972; Chung Chi College was located on the new campus earlier.

Terms of Reference for U.G.C. Hong Kong

U.G.C. is charged with the responsibility to keep under review in the light of the community's needs (a) the facilities for university education in Hong Kong; (b) such plans for development of the universities as may be required from time to time; (c) the financial needs of university education; (d) and to advise the government on the application of such funds as may be approved by the legislature for university education.[2]

The Hong Kong Government has been rather specific in indicating to U.G.C. the level of university teaching and research which it would be willing to support. This determination has been made both with respect to student enrollment and finance. The government has been equally explicit in indicating to U.G.C. particular types of graduates which it would like to see the universities produce in order to meet the needs of the community.

---

2. *Ibid.,* p.3.

University Autonomy

U.G.C. in Hong Kong has recognized five basic areas in which autonomy should operate.[3]

First, selection of staff. Whatever may be the formalities of such things as appointments and procedures for agreeing on pay-scales, a university should have unfettered rights in the actual selection and dismissal of its staff.

Second, selection of students. Although there are many variables that can control the availability of students, the university should be free to select or reject students taken from the available source.

Third, control of curricula and academic standards. This implies constant and continuous examination of the local system of primary and secondary education and further education facilities, but it is essential that the university, after consideration of all local conditions, should exercise final decisions on its own curricula and standards.

Fourth, acceptance of research programs. In considering the right to reject or accept research programs, community needs and problems must be given great weight, but in the last resort the university is likely to be the best judge of whether its combined resources of men, equipment, and money can in fact be deployed in the manner required.

Fifth, allocation of money within the university.

The determination of the size of the block grant is a matter of considerable complexity, requiring detailed reports and justifications from the universities and careful evaluations of the requests against community needs on the part of U.G.C., financial resources always being a basic limitation. The process of decision making on such a complex problem should be enhanced by combining, on the same board, professionals who know the technical aspects of university programs and business leaders from the community whose personal concern is to make certain that community needs are met within the available resources for higher education.

Significant consultation takes place between the U.G.C. and the Government of Hong Kong. However, the final decision involves certain prohibitions and suggestions which U.G.C. and the government transmit to the universities along with the announcement of the

3. *Ibid.*, pp. 4-5.

block grant. It is within this framework that the universities are free to spend the grant as they consider proper during the period for which it is available.

It is clear, in the published reports of U.G.C. that the committee and the executive secretary are determined to prevent unnecessary duplication of programs between the two universities. One reason for this is that the combined enrollments of the two universities was approximately 5,000 students in 1970 and is expected to rise to about 6,000 by 1974.

THE PROCESS OF DETERMINING OPERATING BUDGETS

The secretary of U.G.C. indicated the procedures by which the recurrent-grant recommendations for 1970-74 were made. In March 1968, a timetable of events, the principal issues and the various forms and returns were discussed with the universities. Initial work was carried out in Hong Kong, followed by a meeting of U.G.C. in London in August 1968. The committee's requirements were immediately transmitted to the universities. The meeting of U.G.C. to discuss the quadrennial grants with universities was scheduled for March 1969. U.G.C.'s recommendations to the government were ready by October or November 1969; and government decision was reached by the end of the calendar year 1969. This gave the universities about six months notice before the quadrennium actually started. This is undoubtedly one of the most significant aspects of the whole system.

POLICIES AND PROBLEMS OF U.G.C.

U.G.C. in Hong Kong has assisted the universities in developing significant policies for higher education. These included tuition and fees, and student-staff ratios. There has been a tendency, according to U.G.C., to overrate the significance of student-staff ratios. They are neither the only nor the best measure of a university's strength. Although the committee did not place into operation a staffing formula for Hong Kong universities, it did indicate that there should be some restriction on the proportion of senior appointments.

There has been a careful analysis of unit cost per student and per graduate, taken department by department for the determination of block grants. But the committee did not regard unit costs as decisive within themselves.

Research is an increasing concern in the universities. The committee has been guided by the hypothesis that students cannot be introduced to the body of existing knowledge without reference to the discovery of new knowledge. The committee rejected the idea that outside agencies rather than the government should assume the financial responsibility for research, because teaching and research are interdependent in the university.[4]

EVALUATION BY THE VICE-CHANCELLOR

The Vice-chancellor of the University of Hong Kong indicated positive advantages resulting from the U.G.C. system. Although only three years old, as of 1970, U.G.C. had influenced the universities to assume more autonomy and more responsibility. The block grant for three years, which was changed to a four-year grant for the second period, makes it necessary for the vice-chancellor, his faculty, and assistants to set priorities, to determine how much shall be spent for each department and for each faculty. Previously the universities bargained directly with the government on an annual basis and it was easy for the vice-chancellor to pass the buck to the government and say, "There is no money for anything not specifically approved and funded by the government." Now the funding is in a block grant and university authorities cannot escape the responsibility for using the funds and making decisions with respect to priorities.

U.G.C. has influenced policies regarding tuition and fees, student-faculty ratios, proportion of faculties teaching undergraduates, unit costs, research, buildings and equipment, libraries, extracurricular programs, duplication of academic programs, student and faculty housing, centralized data processing, and long-range plans for the amalgamation of three colleges into one university. These policies have been developed with community needs as the paramount criterion.[5]

The U.G.C. in Hong Kong is similar to a board of trustees that controls two or three universities in the United States. However, there is one important difference. In Hong Kong, the U.G.C. bridges

---

4. *Ibid.*, pp. 19-20.
5. *Ibid.*, pp. 18-19.

the gap between the universities and the government. University officials do not bargain with political leaders for the higher education budget.

NEW ZEALAND—A NATIONAL SYSTEM OF HIGHER EDUCATION

Provision for Higher Education

The University of New Zealand was established in 1870. Its functions were limited to those of an examining body since there were no universities. The functions were changed in 1926 to comprise four university colleges. They were Auckland University College, founded in 1882; Victoria University College of Wellington, founded in 1897; Canterbury University College at Christchurch, founded in 1873; and University of Otago at Dunedin, founded in 1869.

In 1959, New Zealand approached the problem of national participation in university issues by having an international committee study the problems and recommend government action.

The minister of education appointed the Committee on New Zealand Universities. It consisted of three members plus two distinguished leaders from New Zealand education, who served as joint secretaries to the committee. They were as follows: Sir David Huges Parry, Emeritus Professor of English Law and director of the Institute of Advanced Legal Studies, University of London who served as chairman; Dean Geoffrey C. Andrew, deputy to the president of the University of British Columbia, and Roy W. Harman, chairman of New Zealand Council for Technical Education. The joint secretaries were: F.W. Holmes, professor of economics, Victoria University of Wellington, and R.G. Rowley, officer for higher education, Department of Education, Wellington.

In his letter to members of the committee, the minister of education indicated the frame of reference which should guide the committee. He stated:

> The committee is asked to indicate ways in which the university system should be organized to ensure that the long-term pattern of development is in the best interests of the nation and, without limiting the broad scope of its reference, to inquire into such matters as:
>
> 1. The role of the university in the New Zealand community.

2. The number of young people for whom university education should be provided and the standard of attainment considered desirable for those wishing to enter the universities.
3. The maintenance, extension, and coordination of university education and facilities.
4. Recruitment, staffing, and conditions of employment in universities.
5. The financial needs of university education and appropriate means of providing for those needs.
6. Any other matters relevant to university education in New Zealand.

These topics represent only a few of the large number that could be suggested, but the government would prefer that the committee consider itself free to give advice on other matters where it feels it can be of help.[6]

The committee received submissions from 138 individuals and organizations. Five serious university problems emphasized by the committee were: staffing, buildings, conditions of study, university government, and finance. The committee report noted:

We also think that, if our recommendations relating to university government are adopted, it will be important in the national interest that a University Grants Committee should be constituted by an Act of Parliament without delay and before the universities become separate institutions.[7]

The Act of 1961 established the University Grants Committee as a corporate body whose membership included the chairman as the chief executive officer and administrative head of its organization; four members from outside the universities; and three members each of whom was to be a professor or a teacher in a university.

The chairman of the U.G.C. is appointed by the governor-general after consultation between the minister of education, the chancellors and vice-chancellors of the universities, and the principals of university colleges of agriculture. Unless the chairman is removed from office or resigns or dies, he continues in office until age sixty-five.

The governor-general appoints the other seven members of U.G.C. from a panel submitted to the minister of education by a conference presided over by the chairman of the U.G.C. Other members of the conference are the chancellor and vice-chancellor of each of the universities, and the principal of each of the university colleges of agriculture. Although the minister of education may call for a panel as

---

6. *Report of the Committee on New Zealand Universities* (Wellington: Government Printing Office, 1960), p. 5.
7. *Ibid.*, p. 4.

large as he desires, he is under no obligation to submit to the governor-general a panel any larger than the number of vacancies.

Members of the U.G.C. other than the chairman serve for a term of five years and may be reappointed for a second five-year term. A member who has served two terms is not eligible for reappointment until after a lapse of one year during which he has not been a member of U.G.C.

No member of U.G.C. is permitted to vote on any question before that committee or any subcommittee thereof in which he has a direct pecuniary interest.

RESPONSIBILITIES OF THE CHAIRMAN OF U.G.C.

The chairman of U.G.C. is the chief executive officer of that agency which coordinates the functions of all universities and university colleges in New Zealand. By virtue of his office, he is a member of every subcommittee of U.G.C. and in all cases where he is present for meetings of such subcommittees, it is mandatory that he serve as chairman of such meetings. In 1970, he was chairman of the Curriculum Committee, the Research Committee, and the Universities Entrance Board.[8]

A fourth important committee, although not under U.G.C., is the Vice-Chancellors' Committee. It is composed of the vice-chancellors of the universities and the principals of the university colleges of agriculture.

U.G.C., its subcommittees, and the Vice-Chancellors' Committee are all creatures of Parliament created by the Act of 1961, and have clearly delineated functions as specified in that Act.

THE FUNCTIONS OF U.G.C.

The functions and powers of the University Grants Committee are as follows:[9] (1) to collect and publish information relating to university education and research; (2) to analyze the needs of New Zealand for university education and research; (3) to study the financial needs of university education and research, including the recurring and

---

8. *Universities, An Act to Make Better Provision for the Advancement of University Education in New Zealand* (Universities Act 1961), p. 18.
9. *Ibid.,* pp. 7-18.

nonrecurring financial needs; (4) to initiate and consider, in consultation with the universities and other bodies, plans for such balanced university development as may be required to make the universities fully adequate to the needs of New Zealand; (5) to determine the allocation of grants of money to be recommended by it for appropriation by Parliament to meet the needs of university education and research; and to review universities' expenditures of money appropriated by Parliament; (6) to advise and make recommendations to the Government of New Zealand through the minister of education on any matters relating to university education and research requiring the consideration of the government; (7) to provide secretarial and administrative services for the Universities Entrance Board, the Curriculum Committee, the Research Committee, the Vice-Chancellors' Committee, and the Council of Legal Education; (8) to provide secretarial and administrative services for such other committees, bodies, and conferences as the U.G.C. may decide; (9) to perform and exercise all other functions and powers conferred on it by the government.

Every application by any university for any grant by the government of money or property must be made to the U.G.C. Moreover, the council of each university must submit to the U.G.C. for approval any academic development which may lead to a request to the U.G.C. for a special grant to support that development or any extension thereof.

In cooperation with the minister of finance, U.G.C. has the responsibility for investing trust funds or endowments or any money belonging to or vested in the U.G.C. and available for investment.

Finally, U.G.C. has the authority to require the council of every university to supply it with all the information it considers necessary for the effective discharge of its duties.

At the end of each year, U.G.C. is required to furnish to the minister of education a report with respect to the operations of the committee during the preceding year together with a copy of the report of every university for that year. This same report, including those from the universities, must be laid before Parliament within twenty-eight days after the date on which they are furnished to the minister of education if Parliament is then in session, or in any case within twenty-eight days after Parliament commences the next session.

FUNCTIONS OF IMPORTANT U.G.C. COMMITTEES[10]

The Curriculum Committee

The council of each university is mandated to submit to the Curriculum Committee any proposed course regulations with an explanation of changes.

Course changes involving any academic development which in the opinion of the council of the university submitting the changes or in the opinion of the Curriculum Committee require a special grant to support such developments must be approved by U.G.C.

Research Committee

Out of money received for the purpose of research, U.G.C. acting through the Research Committee, makes research grants and authorizes the expenditure of sums for the purpose of encouraging research in New Zealand or elsewhere. Grants are made to specific persons for specific purposes by way of research fellowships, assistantships, and funds for the purchase of special equipment or materials.

Although there is necessarily keen competition for research grants, in a recent year fifty-one grants ranging from $460 to $20,000 were made to the University of Canterbury staff. Other sources of research funds are the Medical Research Council, the Carnegie Corporation, the national lottery and departmental funds.

The Universities Entrance Board (U.E.B.)

The U.E.B. is a significant body in determining the thresholds of admission to the universities. The 1961 University Act gave the Entrance Board the following functions or powers: to establish and maintain a common educational standard as a prerequisite for university entrance; to prescribe the conditions of examinations for university entrance and scholarships; to prescribe regulations that permit exceptions from university entrance examination; to issue certificates to persons who pass the examinations; to award bursaries and scholarships on the results of scholarship examination and to make regulations governing the number, value, and other conditions of any such bursaries and scholarships.

---

10. *Ibid.,* pp. 21-22.

FUNCTIONS OF THE
VICE-CHANCELLORS' COMMITTEE[11]

The 1961 Universities Act made the Vice-Chancellors' Committee a legal body but hardly did justice to the functions of the committee. Other committees, including U.G.C., are mandated to confer with the universities on virtually all important matters. The vice-chancellors, as a group and individually, have tremendous influence, albeit informal rather than legal, upon the development of policies and procedures affecting the universities and upon the allocation of funds to support university functions.

PROCEDURES OF U.G.C.[12]

The U.G.C. maintains a secretariat in Wellington with adequate professional, administrative, and clerical personnel to carry out its functions. The chairman of the committee is a full-time administrator in charge of the secretariat.

Recurring grants (e.g., operating funds) to the universities are made on a quinquennial basis. Nonrecurring (capital) grants are made on an annual basis. Near the end of the fourth year of each quinquennium, U.G.C. and its professional staff submit to the government a proposal for the recurring expenses for the ensuing quinquennium. Although the procedures in determining the amount of the block grant may vary, a few specific steps have become a standard part of the process. First, there is a review of each annual report showing the pattern of expenditures for each of the universities. This gives U.G.C. an opportunity to determine whether block grants in general have been used to implement programs submitted for the previous quinquennium. This also entails an appraisal of whether or not earmarked grants have been used for purposes indicated in the original request from the universities and to carry out any specific programs requested by the government.

Second, there is a review of new developments, programs, and curricula as submitted by the universities. These may involve expansion of existing academic programs, the addition of new departments or faculties, and research activities. New developments are scruti-

11. *Ibid.*, p. 29.
12. Based upon interviews with Chairman and staff of U.G.C. in Wellington.

nized very carefully by U.G.C. because once a new program is approved as a part of recurring expenses, it tends to represent a permanent increase in the operating budget. The chairman tends to encourage faculties and vice-chancellors to squeeze out of the quinquennial block grant most of the resources or funds needed for support of research. Therefore, research has a much lower priority, at least within the policies of U.G.C., than teaching.

Third, there is a careful review of problems, pressures, and budgetary shortages of the previous five years. This provides an excellent opportunity for program planning for five years into the future based upon the previous quinquennium. To prepare for these reviews, U.G.C. and its professional staff, throughout the previous quinquennium, make visits to the various universities, confer with university councils, professors and administrators. The Vice-Chancellors' Committee, representing all of the universities, and each vice-chancellor, representing his own, make submissions to U.G.C. setting forth their views for programs and support.

The final step in the determination of the quinquennial request is for U.G.C. and its professional staff to develop a total budget for all universities for the first and fifth years of the quinquennium. A straight line is then drawn between these two figures and the recurring grant for each year of the quinquennium is located on that continuum.

Academic and administrative salaries are determined each year. Variations in salaries may change the amount of the recurring grant for any given year and require supplementary government grants. However, there is a tendency to negotiate salaries for a three-year period. In 1970, the chairman of U.G.C. was chairman of the Salaries Committee.

Projections indicated that enrollment would increase by forty percent and recurring expenses by eighty-three percent for the quinquennium 1970-74 over the previous five-year period. The operating budget was $18,800,000 for 1969-70, and the enrollment 29,209, which meant that the universities had approximately $643 per student for operating funds. Recurring grants were expected to rise to $34.4 million, plus any salary increases, by 1974. Enrollments, which have been increasing ten percent annually, were expected to reach 42,000 by 1974.

GRANTS FOR BUILDING PROGRAMS

Capital grants are not provided on a quinquennial basis. Indeed, there is no fixed amount provided on an annual basis. Building programs are considered at any time that the vice-chancellor and council of a university present a request to U.G.C. However, university projects are in competition with all other public building programs. There is one public building fund for the entire country and universities have their claims for capital expenditures evaluated alongside those that come from other agencies of government.

Each individual project must be submitted to U.G.C. at many stages, then to the Public Works Committee for approval of preliminary sketches; then working drawings must be submitted, and the final drawings must be submitted both to U.G.C. and to the Public Works Committee.

These procedures make long-range planning for building programs extremely difficult. The procedure may impede desirable progress toward completion of a building program even though the decision has been made to go ahead. For example, in 1948, the decision was made to move the University of Canterbury, which existed on a site of five acres more or less in the center of Christchurch, to a new site of 170 acres which is about three miles out. The move will be completed in 1973, or twenty-five years after the decision was made.

CONCLUSIONS

It is reasonable to say that the universities have the initiative on what they will do within the quinquennial block grant. Indeed, they have great freedom to use the recurring grant with very little interference from U.G.C. However, the approval of new courses and departments must be submitted to the Curriculum Committee which is under the control of U.G.C.

It is possible that the composition of U.G.C. poses a problem in university representation at the point where most important decisions are made. For example, there are six universities and university colleges of agriculture but there are only three university teachers on U.G.C. Although each representative is expected to represent all universities rather than his own, there is probably a greater tendency to represent one's own university than would be the case if the unrepresented outnumbered the represented universities. The problem here is to select university representatives as well as the four laymen who are of such stature, national vision and commitment as to place the interests and concerns of the total universities and the society above any one part.

U.G.C. is in a position to place a definite limitation upon operating budgets. Moreover, the budget going to each university is never a matter of public knowledge. Only the total grants to all universities are announced. No university could find out from U.G.C. what any other university secured in the way of recurring grants. U.G.C. places a limitation upon university expansion by virtue of its interlocking relationship with the U.E.B. The control here is one that is shared by the minister of education who appoints five members of the board, the other five being appointed by U.G.C. after consultation with the Vice-Chancellors' Committee.

By determining admissions standards, building programs, academic expansion, salaries, and operating budgets, U.G.C. and the government definitely limit university expansion to areas deemed essential to the national interests. Public policy determines broad programs and levels of support for higher education. New Zealand is an excellent example of how any one of the fifty states in the U.S. could be organized to develop and implement public policy for higher education.

THE UNIVERSITY GRANTS COMMISSION OF INDIA—NATIONAL AND STATE COOPERATION

Geographically, India is approximately the size of Europe excluding the U.S.S.R. Its area is 1,177,061 square miles and the population is over 400,000,000. The distance from East to West and from North to South is each approximately 1,900 miles.

Historically, political power has been highly decentralized as evidenced by the fact that under British rule there were almost 600 states which included only one-third of the territory of India and one-fourth of the population. With the achievement of independence, in 1947, the principal power was retained by the Indian states; however, it was generally understood that each one would become subordinate to one or the other of the governments of India and Pakistan depending upon the local geography.

The caste system and the concomitant inequity in the distribution of wealth had created a complex hierarchy based upon economics, class, social position, and caste. Adding to the complexity of the hierarchy, and to a certain extent capitalizing upon it, was the British civil service system which found it easier to deal with the multiplicity of states, each comparatively weak, than to run the risk of a strong central government which might have terminated British rule much earlier.

Language was another problem that militated against unity within the new nation. Although Hindi was proclaimed the national language, it was agreed that English would be used for a period of fifteen years as the official language within Parliament, because it was the only one through which people from all parts of the country could communicate.

Education had not been a major concern of the British Government or of the local state governments as far as the masses were concerned. During the period of British rule there was virtually no concern by the government or parents for the education of girls. In 1961 the literacy rate for males was 34.5 and for females 13 percent.

The foregoing conditions made it almost inevitable that education would be developed as a local state function. The contrasts in India, as in almost any developing country, provide the most radical extremes in almost every aspect of the society. There is extreme poverty for the masses and extreme wealth for a limited number of people. The extremes in education range from complete illiteracy for most of the people to sophisticated graduates of Harvard, Cambridge, Oxford and other advanced universities in the world. It is generally agreed that the education of Indian leaders in British universities provided the strongest bulwark of India against the enemies of parliamentary government.

The extremes in agriculture range from the yoke of oxen pulling a plow made of wood to the most sophisticated mechanized farming. The range in production of agricultural products is equally great, depending upon the methods of cultivation and the availability of water resources sufficient for production. Irrigation projects developed by the British constitute one of the most phenomenal contributions ever made to the subcontinent.

Although there is a National Ministry of Education with a Secretary of State for Education, education is a local state function. This is one of many ideas borrowed from the United States system. The U.S. Constitution and the British Parliamentary system were drawn on extensively for guidelines in the writing of the constitution which was adopted on November 26, 1949. It provided for the setting up of parliament, the creation of an independent judiciary with wide powers and a guarantee of fundamental rights.

The Constitution of India represented a compromise between autonomous local states and an all-powerful central government. It is a remarkable tribute to the intellectual and political leaders in India that they have been able to make this system work. It has been necessary for India to move into the forefront of developing nations with extremely limited resources, the second largest population of any nation in the world, and great ideological competition for the loyalties of her citizens. Achievement of independence with such limited violence was a landmark in the history of man. Making the democratic system operate in the face of almost insurmountable difficulties is equally significant.

FUNCTIONS OF U.G.C.

The University Grants Commission in India was established by an act of Parliament in 1956. It is composed of nine members, the chairman of which works full time. Appointments to U.G.C. are for a term of five years. The chairman, in 1970, was a former chief justice of the Supreme Court and professor of history. Most of the members are professionals from the universities. They include three vice-chancellors of universities, the director of an institute of science, the secretary of education in the Government of India, the secretary of the ministry of finance, one layman and two professors. There is a secretary to the University Grants Commission and a small group of civil servants who maintain the headquarters office in New Delhi.

There are eighty universities and over 3,000 colleges in India. With the exception of five national universities, all of them are under the control of state governments somewhat noted for their bureaucratic ministries, not excluding education. Virtually all of the colleges are associated colleges, meaning that they come under the control of the universities.

With this highly decentralized system and the increasing necessity for the Central Government to participate in the support of education, Parliament created the U.G.C. as a bridge between the central government and the universities.

U.G.C. in India has two distinct functions. They are the coordination and improvement of university education. U.G.C. does not have the function, as is the case in other countries operating under the system, of channeling large sums of money to the universities for the support of the general program. The commission places major emphasis upon development grants to the universities and colleges designed for the improvement of physical and academic facilities, particularly those essential for advanced study and research such as libraries. Indicative of the importance attached to education, the Estimates Committee of parliament in 1965-66 noted:

> (1) The low investment in education may make all our developmental expenditures infructuous. . . . (2) Grants to the institutions of higher education should be regulated through the University Grants Commission. In the interest of higher education it should be the responsibility of the University Grants Commission to effect promotion and coordination of all higher education and not university education only.[13]

In its 1966-67 report, the commission stated,

> The commission is of the view that the general policy in various fields of higher education, with special reference to coordination and maintenance of standards, should be vested in one body or agency to ensure a planned and coherent developmennt of the whole educational system. There is so much interaction and overlap between the different sectors of higher education (liberal arts, natural sciences, social sciences, agriculture, medicine, etc.), particularly in the context of the progress of science and technology, that any fragmentation or division of responsibility as regards general policy and coordination of standards is liable to be confusing and harmful to the best interest of education and efficient utilization of our limited resources.[14]

In connection with the problem of maintaining standards, the commission stated,

> It has been repeatedly emphasized that prior consultation with the commission is desirable when new universities are proposed to be established, and when legislation about universities is undertaken. In dealing with principles of university structure, organization and policy, it is necessary to maintain coordination on an all-India level, and full consideration should be given to the views of the commission which is specially concerned with the coordination of higher education on a national basis.[15]

---

13. University Grants Commission, Report for the Year 1966-67, p. 49.
14. *Ibid.,* p. 49.
15. *Ibid.,* p. 48.

The commission has rather limited authority to coordinate the universities or to maintain standards, because seventy-five of the eighty universities are under the control of state governments. However, the commission has used its funds, limited as they may have been, and its influence, which is considerable, to effect innovation and to encourage dynamic and progressive changes.

An excellent illustration of commission influence is the continuing use of development grants designed for improvement and innovation. For the year 1966-67, these grants totaled 19,920,022 rupees. Among important programs which were supported were the following: the construction of hostels for students and staff quarters for faculty; improvement of library and laboratory facilities; the development of postgraduate courses in science, the humanities and social science; the development of textbook libraries; scholarships and fellowships in humanities, science, Arabic, and Persian.

The commission has been especially active in the support of graduate studies. U.G.C. generally pays the entire cost of graduate work for the first five years when a new program has been initiated.

The commission has encouraged assistance from foreign governments as well as international organizations such as UNESCO. In collaboration with the Indian High Commission in the United Kingdom and the British Council, the commission sponsored an exchange of visits by young scientists between India and the United Kingdom. During 1966-67, through a cultural exchange program, thirty-eight professors and leaders came to work in India, twenty-one of them from the U.S.S.R.[16]

In June and July 1966, under a contract with Ohio State University, thirty-three summer institutes for college teachers of science were organized, the funds being provided by USAID and supplemented by U.G.C. in India. USAID provided the services of seventy-nine consultants and commodities worth $15,000 on a grant basis.[17]

Although the commission's own resources for research and development were extremely limited, it was able to capitalize upon voluntary grants from friendly countries associated with the Soviet Union and with the United States as well as funds coming from international agencies.

---

16. *Ibid.,* p. 45.
17. *Ibid.,* p. 16.

Early evidence of the commission's concern for innovation and improvement was the appointment of review committees for a number of important subjects in the physical and biological sciences, the humanities and social sciences to study existing facilities, syllabi and standards of teaching and research, and to make suggestions for further improvement. Reports of these review committees have been completed and sent to universities on English, social work, sociology, library science, education, political science, philosophy, biochemistry, botany, chemistry, mathematics, Arabic and Persian studies, military science, psychology and economics.

The commission has been active in the improvement of salary scales for college and university professors. Started during the second five-year plan, the scales were revised during the third plan. Substantial grants were paid to the universities and colleges for implementing the plan. The central government of India, in order to encourage state governments to implement scales recommended by the commission, agreed in 1966 to pay eighty percent of the additional expenditures for a period of five years. State governments were required to pay twenty percent during the five years and to assume full responsibility at the end of five years. Teacher improvement has been regarded as a key to increasing standards, especially at the advanced levels.

U.G.C. has used its funds and influence to encourage local states to invest in facilities and programs of special concern to students. These have involved provision for prompt redressing of grievances; improved student housing, health and counseling services, financial assistance to poor but meritorious students; improvement of libraries, laboratories, and classrooms. The commission encouraged greater participation of students in decision-making and programs in which they are involved, so as to avoid the feeling among them that they are not full members of the university community. It was also noted that courses of study, examinations, academic standards and the appointment of teachers are outside of student decisions.

U.G.C. GRANTS FOR 1967-68[18]

Categories of higher education receiving the highest grants in 1967-68 were: improvement of library and laboratory facilities, the

18. Universities Grants Commission, Report for the Year 1967-68, p. 57.

purchase of library books, grants to colleges of Delhi University, student aid, textbook libraries, postgraduate courses in science, and construction of hostels.

Grants to the five central universities, which are supported exclusively by the national government, totaled 75,245,366 rupees.

Major grants went to support scientific education and research, engineering and technology, affiliated colleges and for the humanities. The total for all categories of grants was 281,897,126 rupees. This was $40,271,018 based upon seven rupees to the dollar, and represented an increase of almost $15 million over grants for the previous year.

The total financing of higher education is distributed almost equally between U.G.C., the states, and tuition and fees. This would seem to indicate a budget of slightly over $120 million for the year 1967-68, and a considerable portion, provided by U.G.C., was used for buildings and laboratories. The total enrollment for that same year was 1,918,972 students in universities and institutions deemed to be universities.

DATA COLLECTED BY U.G.C. IN INDIA[19]

The annual report of U.G.C. includes extensive data on students, curricula, research, teaching, housing of students and staff, affiliated colleges, and graduate and undergraduate enrollments by university and by department within each university. Complete data are collected on graduates by university and by department as well as by graduate and undergraduate degrees.

Very adequate data are included on faculties by university, by rank, and the number by department within each university. Staff-student ratios are provided for different types of institutions and by departments. For example the overall staff-student ratio for 1966-67 was 18. It was 14.9 in university colleges and 18.6 in affiliated colleges.

The areas of the curriculum that attracted the largest number of students were: arts curricula, 40 percent; science, 33 percent; commerce, 9 percent; engineering, 6 percent; medicine, 4 percent; agriculture, 3 percent; law, 2.5 percent; and education, 2 percent.

---

19. University Grants Commission, University Development in India (New Delhi, 1966-67).

Fifty percent of the high school graduates in India go to college and one-half of those who enter finish the bachelor's degree. Slightly more than five percent of the total enrollment was at the graduate level. There were more than 100,000 students pursuing graduate work and research throughout the nation.

GENERAL OBSERVATIONS AND CONCLUSIONS

The Indian Planning Commission operates on a five-year period and U.G.C. plans for the universities parallel the Planning Commission in this respect. U.G.C. receives an annual appropriation and makes its grants to the universities on an annual basis. Its support of the five national universities is 100 percent, but there is no more control over the national universities than over state universities.

U.G.C. makes its recommendations for university support to the minister of state for education, but it also has direct access to the minister of finance which gives U.G.C. cabinet status in bargaining for university funds.

Capital funds are provided on a five-year basis and once U.G.C. has approved a building and agreed to finance it, its contribution is 100 percent of the cost of the building.

All of India's 3,000 colleges are affiliated with universities. Unfortunately, the weakest college tends to set the standard because a given university cannot be more lenient with one college than with the others. There was a general feeling that some colleges should be autonomous in order to have greater freedom for experimentation including the graduation of their own students. Students in affiliated colleges receive their degrees from the parent university.

Equality among the colleges has been emphasized at the expense of quality. The objective of U.G.C. is to try to bring about a balance between the two. This problem of coordination and improvement of standards is a delicate one requiring an academic rather than a political approach. Officials of U.G.C. do not regard control as essential for improvement, i.e., the academic approach is to influence the universities but not to control them. The influence has been an academic one and highly respected by university officials.

For example, visiting committees, for the purpose of studying almost every problem in higher education at the state level, are made up of professionals, generally professors, appointed by U.G.C. There is an obligation to speak the language of academicians rather than bureaucrats. Research on university problems must be carried out by professionals whose only vested interest is the improvement of higher education in India. Officials in U.G.C. and in the universities were cognizant of the fact that the bureaucrat, operating in a formal hierarchy, is motivated in part by allegiance to the hierarchy and what is best for the bureaucracy. This approach to university problems would be absolutely fatal, particularly in view of the limited resources available for higher education in India.

At the same time that U.G.C. is operating from a highly professional or academic frame of reference, each university and its affiliated colleges takes on many of the characteristics of the bureaucracy. Each little system constitutes a hierarchy with the university itself at the apex and very jealous of its position. University presidents resist autonomy for any affiliated colleges, even though their degrees might be awarded by the university itself. In other words, the universities resemble or take on characteristics of the local state in which they operate.

The struggle toward an academic frame of reference in this case is on the part of the national organization, U.G.C., while any tendency toward political interference with the universities is at the state level. Education is a state function, but it is a national concern. It was a national concern for quality higher education that caused U.G.C. to be established.

The secretary of U.G.C. emphasized the principle of striving to achieve coordination and quality through diversity rather than through conformity. The initiative for carrying out this policy is within each university rather than in U.G.C. This is an intelligent recognition of the fact that the government of India, the ministry of education and the U.G.C. are too remote and too limited in personnel and financial resources to interfere directly in the management of 80 universities and 3,000 colleges even if they were naive enough to believe this to be desirable.

I believe that the government of India has been constructive in attempting to improve the ongoing functions of the universities. There is no evidence of the philosophy of instrumentalism (using the universities as instruments for questionable political purposes except at the local state level). State control of universities has militated against any acceptable standards. U.G.C. is attempting to deal with standards without destroying autonomy.

The types of data collected by U.G.C. and the problems of greatest concern are excellent examples of what might be appropriate functions of state councils on higher education in the United States.

References

1. Beaglehole, J.C. The University of New Zealand. Christchurch, New Zealand: Whitcombe and Tombs Ltd., 1937.
2. Bockemuehl, H.W., editor. *New Zealand's Wealth.* New Zealand Geographical Society, Inc. Palmerston North, New Zealand, 1970.
3. Burn, Barbara B., et al. *Higher Education in Nine Countries.* New York: McGraw-Hill Book Company, 1971.
4. Condliffe, J.B. *The Economic Outlook for New Zealand.* Christchurch, New Zealand: Whitcombe and Tombs, Ltd., 1970.
5. *Encyclopaedia Britannica, Inc., Vol. 12.* William Benton, Publisher.
6. University Grants Commission, Report for the Year 1966-67, New Delhi, India.
7. Report of the Education Commission, Education and National Development. Delhi: Government of India Press, 1966.
8. University Grants Commission, Report for the Year 1967-68, New Delhi.
9. University Grants Commission, University Development in India. New Delhi, 1966-67.
10. University Grants Committee of Hong Kong, Report for 1965-68. At the Government Press. Hong Kong, 1968.
11. Universities, An Act to Make Better Provision for the Advancement of University Education in New Zealand, Universities Act, 1961, Wellington, New Zealand.

4

Commonwealth and State Sharing of Responsibility for Higher Education in Australia

The Commonwealth of Australia was established in 1901. Education was made a local state function. The commonwealth has accepted financial responsibility for government schools in its territories. Although education is compulsory from the age of six, the minimum school-leaving age varies from fourteen to sixteen depending upon individual state laws.

The Australian National University and Canberra University College are located in the national capital and are responsibilities of the Commonwealth government. All other universities were created by statutes of state legislatures. Those created in the nineteenth century also have Royal Charters or Royal Letters Patent.

Each of the six states has a university in its capital city. New South Wales, whose capital is Sydney, has five universities: the University of Sydney, the New South Wales University of Technology, and Universities of New England, New Castle and Macquarie. There is a total of fifteen universities.

The distance in miles from the Commonwealth capital of Canberra to the six state capitals and the territorial capital of Tasmania are as follows: Sydney, 150; Melbourne, 290; Hobart, Tasmania, 540; Brisbane, 590; Adelaide, 600; Perth, 1,920; Darwin, 1,950.

Why did the political and university officials of Australia think that the University Grants System of England would work in a country 57.7 times the size of England? Why was there a need for such a national agency? What functions could it perform? Would such an agency improve higher education? Are there social, economic, industrial and human needs that tend to make higher education a commonwealth rather than a provincial problem and concern? Is it possible to work out a satisfactory cooperative relationship between commonwealth and state governments in the support of higher education where education is legally a local function?

These and other questions stimulated this study of Australia. The answers to the foregoing questions should provide insight that could be helpful in solving similar problems that plague the United States, the fifty local states and the universities.

The Australian Universities Commission is the agency that coordinates and evaluates the universities' requests for commonwealth financial participation in their ongoing recurrent and nonrecurrent expenses. In the remainder of this discussion on Australia, A.U.C. will be used to indicate the Australian Universities Commission.

PROCESS BY WHICH A.U.C. WAS ESTABLISHED

On 19 December 1956, the Right Honourable R.G. Menzies, Prime Minister of Australia, wrote a letter to Sir Keith Murray, chairman of the University Grants Committee in Great Britain in which he invited Mr. Murray to study the university problems of Australia. A part of that letter was as follows:

> As foreshadowed in our discussions in London, I have great pleasure in inviting you to head a Committee of Inquiry into the future of the Australian Universities. We would hope that the committee would take a wide charter to investigate how best the universities may serve Australia at a time of great social and economic development within the nation.
>
> The committee is invited to indicate ways in which the universities might be organized so as to ensure that their long-term pattern of development is in the best interests of the nation, and in particular to inquire into such matters as:
>
> (1) The role of the university in the Australian community;
> (2) the extension and coordination of university facilities;
> (3) technological education at the university level; and
> (4) the financial needs of universities and appropriate means of providing for these needs.
>
> This list is not meant to be exhaustive and it does not set out to limit the inquiry to be undertaken by the committee. . .
>
> In brief I have in mind that the committee might pay attention to what Australian universities could reasonably be expected to do, how they might be organized to do this and how their activities should be financed. Some of the specific topics which interest me include: numbers which should be kept in mind in determining whether a new university ought to be established, machinery for ensuring that the creation of new faculties and chairs is done in such a way that existing resources are used adequately and needless duplication does not occur, and an analysis of the adequacy of the Commonwealth Scholarship Scheme whereby some 3,000 new scholarships are available annually for students at tertiary institutions.

These, of course, represent only a few of the large number of topics which could be listed, but I would prefer the committee itself to retain a considerable measure of freedom in deciding which problems might be studied in detail to give the most useful type of advice.[1]

Anyone who understands the early history of Australia and its relationship to England has to admire Prime Minister Menzies for erasing national, international, and colonial boundaries in his decision concerning the chairman of a committee having such grave significance for the future of Australian universities. Moreover, I am particularly impressed with the order in which the prime minister listed the essential problems. He wanted answers to these paramount questions and he stated them in the right sequence:

1. What should the universities do?
2. How should they be organized to do it?
3. How should their activities be financed?

The U.G.C. system of Great Britain is generally rejected in the United States because Great Britain is no larger than one of our fifty states. However, Prime Minister Menzies probably saw the possibility of the transfer from one country to another of basic principles relating to function, organization and support of universities regardless of the geography or population of countries involved.

Australia has transplanted the British U.G.C. to an environment similar to that of the United States, which is what many education leaders in America were doing about 1828 when the Yale Report came out and when the population of the U.S. was about the same as the twelve million that Australia had in 1970.

Sir Keith Murray and the other four members of his committee presented their report to the prime minister in September 1957. The report was accepted and implemented. It became a benchmark in the development of Australian universities. In July 1959, the A.U.C. was established.

FRAME OF REFERENCE AND PROCESS
EMPLOYED BY MURRAY

The Murray Committee was guided by the prime minister's request, however, the committee was free to go beyond specific

1. Sir Keith A.H. Murray, *Report of the Committee on Australian Universities*. Printed and Published for the Government of the Commonwealth of Australia, Canberra, 1957, p. 127.

instructions and to exercise its own initiative in analyzing problems which seemed relevant to the report.

The process by which the committee collected its data and gained insight regarding higher education was unique. The committee went beyond administrators and faculties and invited individuals to submit their views in writing. Specific invitations to make submissions were sent to state governments, universities and organizations involving every aspect of the Australian society. Moreover, there were press releases and news announcements that extended the invitation to all interested individuals and groups to make submissions in writing.

The committee met with vice-chancellors and visited each university and university college. Discussions were held with governing bodies, professional boards, deans and representatives of nonprofessional staff and students at each university and with officials in state departments of education and state treasuries in each state. Appendix A gives a more complete list of submissions.

NATIONAL PROBLEMS OF DEVELOPMENT

Australia's population is concentrated along the eastern and southeastern coastline and in other regions of relatively high rainfall. The population has increased at a rate of 2.5 percent per annum since 1947. This is one of the highest rates of increase of any country in the world. Natural increases have accounted for 60 percent and immigration for 40 percent.

In the period since the end of the Second World War, there has been a phenomenal growth in Australian industry, particularly in manufacturing. Indeed, the Australian economy has expanded at a more rapid rate than the population. It has been a period of full employment and a rising standard of living. It is estimated that twenty-five percent of the gross annual production is being invested in capital, which is some indication of industrial growth.

Agriculture is still the most important source of wealth in Australia. The application of scientific research is indispensable to the improvement of agriculture, as in any other country. In one period of nine years, during 1948-1957, twenty-two million acres of semiarrid native pasture land were converted to high quality farm pasture through the application of agricultural research.[2]

2. *Ibid.*, p. 13.

The shortage of rainfall is the greatest limitation upon agricultural production in Australia, but this problem lends itself to persistent research in colleges of agriculture and experiment stations, the consequences of which are beyond imagination. Without the application of scientific and technical research to development, vast areas of the continent must remain a barren desert.

Australia is a part of the Asian community through her membership in the Colombo Plan and the Southeast Asia Treaty Organization. Close ties with the Commonwealth of Nations, and close political and economic relationships with the United States demand increasing international sophistication in commerce, military defense, and economic security. There is a growing involvement in diplomatic activities at the regional and international levels.

The analysis and appraisal of increasing international activities on the part of Australia, or any other country with any status in the world, would cause one to conclude that even a strictly national university would be a provincial university in 1970. Universities have, by their nature, been international but now it is also by necessity in serving a modern nation-state.

The growth of the economy of Australia and the problems of higher education are two forces closely related. A growing economy requires a vast array of highly skilled workers. Personnel resources related to capital investment and design and fabrication of equipment are basic to economic development. Moreover, a highly developed intelligence capable of coping with the infinite problems of management and coordination of the factors of production is dependent upon advanced education in the universities.

The rationale for education at all levels is to assist national development and to improve the quality of life for the individual. Statistical studies indicate a direct relationship between the Gross National Product and the proportion of the total population engaged in full-time education in highly developed and in developing countries. For example, in 1958, the United States had nearly 70 percent of the age group from 15 to 19 and 12 percent of those 20 to 24 years of age in school, and GNP was approximately $2,700 per capita. At the other end of the scale, Turkey had approximately 4 percent of the 15 to 19 age group and 1 percent of those 20 to 24 years old in school and her GNP was $200 per capita. The United Kingdom had 18 percent of the age group 15 to 19 and 4 percent of the age group 20 to 24 in school, and the GNP was $1,150 per capita.[3]

The need for graduates in Australia includes technologists, scientists, social scientists, doctors, dentists, agriculturalists, lawyers, economists, graduates of the arts and particularly graduates to teach in the elementary and secondary schools of the commonwealth.

The Australian Institute of Agricultural Sciences and the Commonwealth Scientific and Industrial Research Organization require a considerable number of highly qualified scientists to carry on investigations of diseases which are of the greatest possible significance to national interest and health. Moreover, universities have indicated demands for graduates in engineering, chemistry and physics several times the supply of graduates.

The foregoing discussion, pointing out the relationship between agricultural, industrial, educational, and general economic development are significant elements in the commonwealth's increasing concern for education at all levels, but particularly at the university level.

UNIVERSITY PROBLEMS AND NATIONAL POLICY

In 1957, when the Murray Report was being written, there were nine universities and two university colleges in Australia. The total enrollment was 28,171.

By 1969, there were fifteen universities, including the Australian National University, with a total undergraduate enrollment of 80,146 and 14,215 students working for higher degrees. Total enrollment in 1969 was 94,361.[4] This was an increase of 235 percent in 12 years. In 1957, the total enrollment was 4.8 percent of the population 17 to 22 years of age, while in 1969, the total enrollment was 8.2 percent of the 17 to 22 age group. This rapid growth has been due in large measure to the implementation of the Murray Report. The financial support of the universities in Australia, from the establishment of the University of Sydney in 1850 up to the Second World War, has been essentially a state responsibility. In addition to state support there were private endowments, grants and student fees.

---

3. L.H. Martin, Chairman, *Report of the Committee on Tertiary Education in Australia,* Vol. I, 1964, p. 7.
4. Australian Universities Commission, Fourth Report, Commonwealth Government Printing Office, Canberra, 1969, pp. 11-12.

During and since the Second World War, there has been increasing support from the commonwealth and state governments. Under the new policy established and implemented through A.U.C., commonwealth support for operating costs of the universities increased from $10.57 million in 1958 to $146.68 million in 1969.[5]

There are many university problems in Australia that are regarded as of great national concern. Concerted commonwealth policies are necessary in solving such problems.

1. Growth in the number of universities and in the level of support is a problem that demands commonwealth policy, participation, and financial support. Acceleration of commonwealth support of the operating budgets of the universities has been more than five times as great as acceleration in enrollment. Both state support and student fees have decreased as percentages of operating budgets.

2. The quota of undergraduates to be admitted to higher education is clearly a national concern for two basic reasons—the best interests of society and the quality of life for the individual. A nation must decide whether to develop the full potential of individual talent and skills as a first step toward the development of all other resources, or to remain backward in terms of development with concomitant disproportionate investments in welfare and crime.

The admission of a given student (determination of admission thresholds) is clearly an internal function of any autonomous university. The decision on whether a nation or state will provide such diversified opportunities as to permit all students to study and advance to the level of their abilities and motivation is equally clearly a matter of public policy.

Graduates needed for the Australian economy prompted the Murray committee to suggest that universities be put in a position to accept all those who were qualified and wished to enter, and to give them the facilities and teaching to ensure each of them a reasonable opportunity for graduation.

Part-time and external students require special kinds of opportunities leading to degrees earned over longer periods of time regardless of where such students live and regardless of whether they can attend as residential students.

3. The attrition rate of students is a national concern, an extrav-

---

5. *Ibid.*, p. 40.

agance, a waste of talent, and sometimes a scandal within a given university. The rate is expected to be higher where any high school graduate can enter the university, but there was a strong argument for graduating eighty percent under the nonselective admissions policy in Australia.

4. Graduate education and the number of students completing advanced degrees are of prime national concern, require national planning, priorities and financing.

In proportion to population, Australia, in 1957, was producing one-fourth as many Ph.D.'s as British universities, and only one-fifth as many as universities in the United States and Russia. At that time, the United States was acting as if it would be impossible to produce too many Ph.D.'s in any field or as a total. More careful planning is called for in the interest of students themselves, the national interests and in terms of economy and efficiency in the use of scarce resources. For example, adequate planning and ordering of priorities in the United States would not have found the nation, in 1971, with vast surpluses of Ph.D.'s in the sciences and such scandalous shortages of paraprofessionals as well as M.D.'s in the health sciences.

The Australian National University was established in 1946. Its prime responsibility was research and graduate studies of fundamental importance from a theoretical as well as a national frame of reference. During its first ten years, only students who were candidates for the Ph.D. were admitted.

5. Buildings and expensive equipment are state-wide, and in small countries, national problems. Duplication of facilities and expensive equipment within a state or even a region comprising several states, is not in the best interest of higher education. Public policy that transcends all universities is indicated to promote the highest quality education and to guard the public interest against unnecessary duplication and overbuilding in terms of fundamental needs. In Australia, it was recognized that sixteen percent of the construction cost of a building should be made available for equipment.

6. Another problem that is of great concern to A.U.C. is the need to review university salaries on a national basis. Such an advisory group should include a fair representation from within the universities.

Salaries, retirement and fringe benefits should follow a common pattern as to criteria and levels for similar positions within a state or nation where support is provided by taxes. Yet one must admit that in large state universities in the United States, there is sometimes a radical difference among schools and colleges within the same university or among departments within a given school on matters of salary levels. Policies come close to being capricious. One is forced to raise the question of whether a state should leave such important morale factors to the whims of deans, vice presidents and presidents. Salary levels and retirement programs should make it easy for professors to transfer from one university to another and from one state to another without loss of status.

7. The problem of scholarships and grants to students has been recognized as a commonwealth problem and concern in Australia. Left to local agencies of government, scholarship programs tend to place serious restrictions upon students such as bonding them to work for local education authorities or engineering firms. Moreover, many students receive scholarships to study outside of Australia. This was an important item of policy and expenditure in every country studied in connection with this research.

The United States is somewhat backward in providing budgeted scholarships for American students to study abroad. There is probably no nation in greater need of such enrichment, because Americans are not noted for understanding or appreciating foreign cultures. We are noted chiefly for trying to recast them by an American mold.

8. Radical differences in the costs of different departments within universities provided part of the rationale for A.U.C.-directed policies in Australia. It was learned, for example, that the cost per student in the faculty of law at the University of Sydney was one-sixth the cost per student in engineering; and at Melbourne the same costs had a ratio of one to ten, and the cost per student in history was one-half as much as in chemistry.

9. Australia recognized four levels of professional and technological education: (a) engineering and applied science; (b) the technologist; (c) the technician; (d) the tradesman.

Industry can absorb five or six technicians for every technologist. Throughout Australia the programs of education for engineers and applied scientists and for technicians and craftsmen are clearly defined and understood, but there are many problems yet to be solved in the education of a very large group of professional and subprofessional personnel between the two extremes.

The solution of the problem of scientific and technical education requires cooperation between local states, individual universities, the commonwealth, industry, and agriculture toward the development of the nation's resources. Moreover, it was evident that serious imbalances may develop between the relative emphasis given to scientific and technical education compared to the arts and humanities.

10. The establishment of new universities was recognized as a policy on which A.U.C. should exercise a very strong influence. There was a strong suggestion that the upper limit of enrollment in a given university should not exceed 12,000 students.

The establishment of a graduate school for Business Administration became a very important national decision. To perform an advisory role on this last problem, four experts were invited from the United States. They spent one month during February and March 1970, in reaching a decision summarized in a Report of the Committee of Inquiry into Postgraduate Education for Management.

The central parts of the committee's recommendations are given in the following paragraphs.

Eighty-seven individuals and organizations made written submissions to the above committee; twenty-two universities and colleges and nineteen other organizations were visited; and 274 individuals, representing business, industry and the professions, were interviewed by the committee.

> Our conclusion that a single national school be established led us to the thorny problem of selecting a location for it. Melbourne and Sydney, with their concentrations of people, universities and industry are both equally suitable sites and both communities were equally receptive.
>
> We then turned to other criteria for selecting the university for the proposed national school. The criteria were a commitment to management education, an understanding of the quality and role of the national school and an appreciation of the organizational conditions under which such a school might thrive and serve its intended purpose. We, therefore, sought to identify that university which offered the highest likelihood of meeting these criteria. On this basis one university stood out from the others. Its proposals clearly met the criteria. In particular we were impressed by the fact that the vice-chancellor, the dean, and the senior staff members all recognized that the new school could not be grafted onto the existing

faculty, but would have to be given a fresh start. This was the University of New South Wales.[6]

Accordingly we recommended that development of the national school in the University of New South Wales should proceed along with the tangible encouragement of promising programs in other universities.[7]

RATIONALE FOR AUSTRALIAN UNIVERSITIES COMMISSION[8]

Having reviewed the problems of higher education as related to economic and social development in Australia, I now come to a review of why the Australian Universities Commission was established.

Leaders in the commonwealth and state governments, in the universities and in private organizations representing business, industry, and the professions in Australia seemed to have been in agreement (in 1957) on two fundamental principles regarding higher education. First, they recognized higher education as a national concern, absolutely necessary to the economic, social, agricultural, industrial and cultural development of the commonwealth and its people. Second, they recognized the fact that universities and their scholars can perform their most important tasks only in an atmosphere of freedom, and without political interference.

University autonomy combined with purposes, functions, programs, curricula, research and experimentation adequate to national needs was not viewed as a metaphysical contradiction.

It was clearly recognized that universities responsive to concerted national concerns did not preclude diversity among them. On the contrary, national interests mandated diversity and the avoidance of the expensive duplication of highly specialized programs.

In addition, it was acknowledged that universities should find a way to speak as a group in making their concerns known to governments. Competition among universities makes concerted action on their part impossible. There was no disposition to exclude universities and their representatives from active participation in determining concerted national policy. However, it was clear that conse-

---

6. Report of the Committee of Inquiry into Post-Graduate Education for Management, Australian Government Publishing Service, Canberra, 1970, p. 8.
7. *Ibid.*, p. 9.
8. Murray, *op. cit.*, pp. 97-107.

quences of higher learning and research impinge upon all sectors of a society.

It was noted that universities must always be selective in regard to their functions, because no group of imaginative professors and their leaders can ever hope to secure the financial resources to implement all requests emanating from pressure groups and from their own initiative.

The above factors pointed to the necessity for the needs of all universities as a group and those of each individual university to be objectively considered within available resources for higher education. It was necessary to find a process of making decisions on the allocation of resources that would *avoid a competitive approach on the part of universities and avoid government decisions based upon political pressure.*

The judgment of university people with respect to their needs should be paramount with governments, providing there is agreement among universities and response to the needs of society. The objective on the part of Murray and his committee was to find a way to unite academic expertise with the knowledge of public affairs and "business good sense." A strictly lay policy group would not be adequate. Neither would a commission made up exclusively of academic personnel.

There were specific problems of Australian universities and of the commonwealth that pointed to the need for a more rational and objective approach to the support and coordination of university activities. Ten of those problems were noted in the previous section. Other specific reasons for A.U.C. included:

1. Internal university organization tended to dichotomize academic affairs and financial support with the vice-chancellor's role confined largely to the latter as is the case with most university presidents in the United States.

2. Increasing emphasis upon research, coordination of university research activities with those of the Commonwealth Scientific and Industrial Research Organization and the Nuclear Research Foundation and the general explosion of knowledge demanded careful delineation of responsibilities and allocation of financial resources.

3. Universities cannot be adequate to contemporary societies and remain provincial or even national. By nature, they are international and serve as a strong force in developing regional and world communities.

4. Universities needed to be relieved of the hand-to-mouth existence by which local states were supporting them if they were to fulfill long-range national and international responsibilities.

5. Existing problems as well as the promise of more viable universities pointed to the desirability for an agency to present university needs to the government and to keep the concerns of society within university programs.

6. Such an agency would serve as a buffer or bridge or connecting link between universities and the political arena. It would spare universities the necessity of competing with one another before legislative and executive political authorities. The Australian Universities Commission would need to enjoy the confidence of commonwealth and state governments, the general public and the universities.[9] It was established as a commonwealth body but separate from the ministry of education.

COMPOSITION OF THE COMMISSION

Murray recommended that the Commission be composed of representatives from five groups of disciplines: arts, social sciences, pure sciences, applied sciences (including engineering), and medicine and dentistry. These academic members should be persons of wide university experience, or high scholastic repute and capable of taking a broad view of the universities' responsibilities in the community.[10] Murray noted in this connection:

> The understanding of university affairs, the differences in outlook, philosophy and future of the many disciplines which constitute a full university, the delicacy of the balance between them, the complexities of academic status and staff structure, and above all the need for the maintenance of academic freedom appear to us to be good reasons for strong academic representation on the committee, as members and not merely as assessors.[11]

It was recommended that the commission be composed of a full-time chairman, with personal experience in university affairs, and seven part-time members, of whom two would be lay members from the professions or industry and five would be academic members, competent to consider university problems on a broad basis but also to provide particular knowledge throughout the many fields of uni-

---

9. *Ibid.,* p. 104.
10. *Ibid.,* p. 104.
11. *Ibid.,* p. 105.

versity interest. The members of the commission would be chosen for their individual capacity, and would not serve as representatives of governmental, academic or any other partisan interest. Since 1965, the commission has included eight part-time members, plus the chairman. Concerning the competence of academic members to serve on such a commission Murray stated:

> Doubts have been expressed whether academic members would be capable of looking at a university as a whole rather than from the view point of their own particular academic interest. We do not accept this view and are confident that men exist in academic circles who can take a broad view of university affairs and who are able to make well-balanced, practicable and reasonable judgments, not only in their own fields but in other disciplines.
>
> It has been represented to us in some quarters that any committee should include representatives of the commonwealth or state governments. We think that it would be wrong in principle and embarrassing in practice if any advisory body designed to give objective advice to governments included government representatives among its membership.[12]

Great importance was attached to maintaining close liaison with commonwealth and state governments but the point was emphasized that these contacts would be better achieved through the chairman of the commission rather than through membership of government officials on the commission.

It was suggested that one or more vice-chancellors might serve as academic members of the commission. Murray's reaction was that this would put any vice-chancellor in "a most *invidious position* as it would be impossible for anyone in this dual position to disassociate himself from the particular needs of his university."[13]

He did not think that the amount of time involved would present any problem for part-time members. The most serious and time-consuming effort would be the triennial visit to all institutions. It was his judgment that every university should be visited in the opening months of the third academic year. He anticipated that this would involve about six weeks of travel over a period of three months. In addition to the triennial visits to the universities, he anticipated that six to eight meetings of the commission each year, one day for each meeting, would be sufficient to transact commission business and that the full-time chairman and secretariat would be able to fulfill all other responsibilities.

---

12. *Ibid.*, p. 105.
13. *Ibid.*, p. 106.

PROCESS OF OPERATION

The Murray Committee gave the universities, the commonwealth and state governments an example of how such a commission should approach the problem of university buildings. Because the university grants system as proposed could not be implemented immediately, specific recommendations were made regarding building programs for 1958-60.

For each university, specific buildings and costs were recommended. The total building program recommended for the three years came to £12,445,000 with the commonwealth government being asked to assume a little more than fifty percent of the total.[14] The commonwealth contribution was to be £6,270,000. It was recommended that sixteen percent of the commonwealth contribution to the building program be made available for equipment.

In addition to the recommended building program for state universities, the committee asked for £1,070,000 for the Australian National University and £1,044,000 for Canberra College. Both of these items included the sixteen percent for equipment as a part of the total.[15]

The Murray Committee requested the universities to submit their estimates necessary to correct serious deficiencies in staffing and in research and to deal with the enrollment increases anticipated for 1958 through 1960. These were in the nature of recurrent grants. Reactions of committee members to requests in these categories were unique. They stated:

> We have attempted to assess the needs of each university on as realistic a basis as is possible, bearing in mind each one's particular needs and circumstances and also the available manpower resources from which they will have to recruit additional staff. We are convinced that they could not, in the aggregate, spend the sums which they submitted to us as necessary in the immediate future but we believe they could deal effectively and usefully with an additional sum of £1,015,000 in 1958, £1,522,000 in 1959, and £2,030,000 in 1960.[16]

Murray and his committee did not believe that the states could respond to this emergency need with the speed which seemed necessary if the universities were not to collapse under the weight of increasing numbers of students. He said, "We therefore recommend

---

14. *Ibid.,* p. 113.
15. *Ibid.,* p. 115.
16. *Ibid.,* p. 118.

that the Commonwealth government should provide the entire funds for this emergency period."

For the three-year building program, the Murray Committee recommended approximately fifty percent of what the universities requested. Although the recommendation for recurrent grants was substantially less than the universities requested, it represented major improvements on an emergency basis and served as an example of commonwealth response that could be effective and quicker than state response.

I believe that both commonwealth and state governments felt more comfortable about the requests for building programs and for recurrent grants than they would have if the universities individually had presented their requests to state and commonwealth governments without the objective consideration on the part of the Murray Committee which coordinated the total request in terms of an overall national need.

Assuming that the requests would have gone to the six state governments, the government of Tasmania, and the commonwealth government, there would have been a minimum of eight governmental agencies attempting to make the necessary reductions in the requests without any effective coordination between the eight agencies.

REGULAR RECURRING GRANTS FROM 1958 THROUGH 1960

In making recommendations for recurrent grants for the three-year period, the Murray Committee illustrated the process by which A.U.C. would arrive at a decision on such an important aspect of the budget. The committee noted that recurrent grants are much more difficult to determine than building needs because the university is so complex that the allocation of recurrent income can be made only by the university itself in the light of circumstances that change almost daily.

Although the Murray Committee did not choose to be specific in the allocation of operating funds as it had been in the case of capital funds, it did make certain observations in order that the universities would understand why increases in operating funds had been recommended.

Among the reasons given for increases in operating funds were the need for the improvement in staff-student ratios, particularly in departments where teaching loads were abnormally heavy. This applied especially to departments of history, English, psychology, mathematics, chemistry, and physics. It was suggested that additional appointments of staff should be made as qualified individuals became available. There was a concern for the lack of development of honors and postgraduate work in some faculties and departments and therefore the universities were encouraged to increase emphasis upon this type of work. There was evidence of inadequate departmental maintenance, equipment of laboratories and book purchases for libraries.

INTERVIEW WITH THE SECRETARY OF THE A.U.C.

In addition to the chairman, A.U.C. has a small secretariat that works full time. The headquarters office is in a bank building in Canberra.

Requests for recurrent and capital grants are submitted by university officials to the A.U.C. approximately two years before Parliament and the Commonwealth Cabinet act on the triennial grant.

Preparation of the requests for the triennium begins with filling out of forms, provided by the commission, starting three years before the grants are made. In a sense, therefore, the universities are always planning six years in advance, the first three being the implementation of the triennial program just approved, and a second three-year period involving advance preparation and justification for recurrent and capital grants for the subsequent triennium.

Visits to the universities by members of the commission are thorough enough for the commission as a whole to really know what is going on in the universities.

There is generally no great problem about recurring grants for ongoing programs plus a small increase (perhaps five percent annually) to take care of increased costs, economic growth and inflation.

Improvement in existing programs in the form of additional staff, equipment, and physical facilities and expansion or addition of curricula, particularly new faculties, are significant matters on which A.U.C. exercises major coordinating control. The new Graduate School of Business Administration, mentioned earlier, is an example of such a problem and how it gets resolved. It would have been impossible to reach this decision without the A.U.C. or a similar organization that represented the commonwealth as a whole rather than having each state settle the issue by establishing six weak Graduate Schools of Business Administration.

AUSTRALIAN RESEARCH GRANTS COMMITTEE

This significant organization has seventeen members including the chairman plus a full-time secretary and a small clerical force located in Canberra. Although considerable research and research training are supported through recurrent grants made by A.U.C. on a triennial basis, highly specialized research projects of great significance to the commonwealth and to the growth of knowledge in various disciplines is under the control of A.R.G.C.

The membership of the committee indicates the fundamental policy of the committee and the process by which it performs its responsibilities. It is a professional group. Practically every member is a professor in one of the Australian universities. In 1969, the chairman was a professor of botany in the University of Adelaide and the other members, in addition to professors from various disciplines and universities, included the chief research chemist from Union Carbide in Australia and a research chemist from the Commonwealth Scientific and Industrial Research Organization.[17]

Terms of Reference of A.R.G.C.[18]

1. Out of financial resources available to the committee, it makes recommendations to the Minister of Education for the support of individuals or groups engaged in particular research projects and this may include the purchase of research equipment.

2. Research projects within the physical, biological, applied and social sciences and in the humanities may be recommended for support.

3. Generally, to be eligible for support, a research project must be carried out in Australia. The committee may recommend an exception to this rule where the nature of the research requires that part of it be performed at a specific place outside Australia.

---

17. Australian Research Grants Committee, Report 1967-69, pp. 2-3.
18. *Ibid.*, pp. 4-6.

4. Only upon the specific approval of the Minister of Education may a research project be eligible for consideration if it is intended to be carried out in a commonwealth or state government agency.

5. Applications for research grants may be made directly to the committee, however, where an application involves a research project to be carried out in a university or other institution, or with facilities to be provided by such an institution, the committee satisfies itself that the institution concerned is aware of the proposal and has an opportunity to comment on it.

6. In determining the relative merits of a particular research proposal, the committee need not have regard to any specific distribution of the amounts recommended among states or among institutions. It bases its recommendation on its own assessment of the relative merits of individual proposals.

7. The committee may consult with the A.U.C. and with other commonwealth research-funding agencies to satisfy itself that overlapping or duplication of support is not occurring. The committee may also refer applications which it has received to other commonwealth research-granting bodies for consideration.

8. The committee must report periodically to the Minister on any proposals referred to it and on the general progress of its activities.

9. The committee may establish its own rules of procedure and is provided with administrative support by the Commonwealth Department of Education and Science.

Two significant criteria have tended to guide the committee in its allocation of research grants.[19] First, the committee has insisted that it be satisfied that there was significant merit in the research proposal. In this regard the committee has tended to direct itself to supporting the most outstanding and promising research being carried out in universities and research institutions. Although the committee has been interested in supporting the most outstanding research being carried on in each discipline, if the work in a particular discipline does not indicate sufficient merit, the committee has resisted all pressure to allocate money for second-rate work even though the discipline itself may be very important.

The second criterion that has guided the committee's allocation of funds involves the qualifications of the individual in charge of each

19. *Ibid.*, p. 8.

research proposal. The committee has to establish for itself that the individual has the skills and all necessary competencies to make a research contribution.

Two criteria enumerated above indicated that the Research Grants Committee was not interested in supporting research training by providing fellowships to graduate students pursuing advanced degrees.

THE FIRST TEN YEARS OF A.U.C.

In May 1969 the commission presented its fourth triennial report which covered the years 1967 through 1969, and recommendations for recurrent and capital grants for the triennium 1970-72.

When this report was completed the commission had been in operation for more than a decade, its first triennium having covered the period 1958-60. The report is significant because it outlines the operational procedures developed over a period of a decade in a country as large as the United States in which education is regarded as a state function as in the United States.

The report of the commission was based upon visits which it made to the universities and university colleges between June and December 1968, other visits made by individual commissioners, and by the chairman and secretary during the triennium.

All universities submitted extensive printed reports to the commission, and the Federation of Australian University Staff Associations submitted a special report on research. The National Union of Australian University Students submitted material on many problems affecting the students. The Vice-Chancellors' Committee made many important suggestions to the commission including the method of calculating recurring grants. Various departments from state and commonwealth governments also cooperated in every way possible with the commission.

In the first ten years under the A.U.C. plan, commonwealth recurrent grants to the universities increased from $10.57 million in 1958 to an average of $133.363 million per annum for the 1967-69 triennium. Both state support and student fees decreased as percentages of the total operating budgets.

Beginning in the triennium 1967 to 1969, commonwealth support of teacher education (capital costs) amounted to $24 million, but operating costs of teacher education continue to be local state responsibility. Denominational teachers' colleges have received governmental financial support since 1955.[20]

Commonwealth financial assistance to students includes awards for fees, tuition and a living allowance (based upon financial need) the latter also varying upward for students living away from home. Approximately 50 percent of all graduate students receive financial aid, the amount being $2,140 for master's degree students and $2,350 for doctoral students in 1968-69.[21]

Special Inquires

One of the special problems of concern to the commission involved the establishment of a fourth School of Veterinary Science in Australia. The commission requested the Commonwealth Department of Primary Industry to make available the services of Dr. R.N. Farquhar to study the advisability of establishing the Veterinary School. Dr. Farquhar recommended that the fourth school of veterinary science be established at the University of New England and that students should be accepted from all states by 1971. The report recommended that there should be between 30 and 40 students in 1971 and that the enrollment should rise steadily until it reached the number which would provide 60 graduates annually.[22]

Other special concerns of the commission included the Vice-Chancellors' Committee report on improved utilization of universities' facilities and the commission's intention to initiate the study of its procedures for analyzing and approving plans for new buildings and alterations to buildings.[23]

Finally, the commission paid particular attention to the relationship between the universities and other resources for tertiary education. It gave special attention to the role of Colleges of Advanced Education and noted that universities in their entrance requirements placed a very great emphasis upon analytical ability and imaginative power and suggested that colleges should, in the opinion of the com-

---

20. Barbara B. Burn, *et al.*, *Higher Education in Nine Countries* (New York: McGraw-Hill Book Company, 1971), p. 148.
21. *Ibid.*, p. 151.
22. A.U.C. Fourth Report, 1969, *op. cit.*, p. 2.
23. *Ibid.*, p. 3.

mission, give more emphasis to practical qualities such as those required for certain managerial positions.[24] However, the commission urged that a liberal policy prevail with respect to transfer of students from advanced colleges of education to the universities and from the universities to advanced colleges of education. It suggested specifically that students from either type of institution be permitted to transfer with appropriate credit for work successfully performed. This liberal transfer policy gave students much greater freedom than has generally prevailed among universities.

Types of Data in the A.U.C. Report

The commission gave a general overview of grants for the previous three triennia and the proposed grants for the triennium beginning in 1970. It included university enrollments as a percentage of the population aged 17-22, going back to 1946 and projecting enrollments to 1972. Enrollments were given for the commonwealth and by state, with projections for the next triennium. Enrollments (undergraduate and graduate) were presented for each university with the total for each state. In each case, previous enrollments, going back at least to 1964, were used as a basis for anticipating the enrollments for the period 1970-72.

Other data presented special enrollments by university. These included individuals working for diplomas, certificates, and other miscellaneous goals of less than a bachelors degree. Wherever there were specific quotas established as a basis for enrollment in various faculties or departments, these were included by university and department.

Student Problems

Included in the report for the previous triennium and as justification for triennial grants for 1970-72 was an impressive list of student problems. Students were concerned about financial assistance to provide Union facilities but the most impressive elements of the student position, submitted by the National Union of Australian University Students, were as follows:

---

24. *Ibid.,* p. 5.

(a) that the commission seek to insure that the minimum student-staff ratios laid down in the 1966 report are achieved and that the commission support proposals for increasing the number of junior academic staff positions, (b) that the commission support proposals for setting up of units concerned with improving teaching and learning in the university, (c) that the commission support proposals for making student welfare services adequate, (d) that the commission recommend grants for additional seating in the university libraries, (e) that the commission recommend grants for the building of low cost student flats.[25]

The commission very wisely noted that it could take an active position with respect to (d) and (e) and suggested that the remainder of the items (a) through (c) were matters for the universities themselves to consider.[26] However, the commission did make note of the fact that the students had made the point that student-staff ratios particularly in large universities needed improvement and that this could best be achieved by the appointment of junior academic staff members whose time would be less occupied with academic administration than that of their seniors.

The commission agreed to request the sum of money sufficient to reduce the student-staff ratios to eleven to one in the larger universities. It noted that the sum was intended not to provide for the additional chairs which many universities wished to create, but to permit the necessary appointments to be made, on an average, at the level of lecturer.

Under the section on student problems, considerable attention was given to foreign students enrolled in the Australian universities. Most of these came from Asia, and the countries of Malaysia, Hong Kong, and Indonesia provided the greatest number of students, accounting for sixty-four percent of all foreign students.

Academic Staff

The commission listed the number of faculty members by rank for each university for the years 1963-66, and 1969. The ranks used were professors; associate professors and readers; senior lecturers; lecturers; senior tutors and senior demonstrators; tutors, demonstrators and teaching fellows. The total teaching staff in 1969 was 7,861, an increase of 6.6 percent over 1968.[27]

---

25. *Ibid.*, pp. 20-21.
26. *Ibid.*, p. 21.
27. *Ibid.*, p. 30.

Although the commission was reluctant to violate its principle regarding the freedom of the universities concerning recurrent grants, it noted that:

> Special sums having been built into recurrent grants for the purpose of improving the student-staff ratio, the commission considers that it would be wrong for that improvement to be regarded as competing with, for example, the creation of new chairs to strengthen specific disciplines. The allocation of funds for such purposes should be regarded as coming after the improvement of the student-staff ratio.[28]

New Developments and Earmarked Grants

The commission sought the views of universities on the question of having the commission recommend earmarked grants. It was the opinion of almost all officials within the universities that earmarked grants were normally undesirable, especially if they grew to large proportions.

> The commission firmly shares that view; the earmarking of recurrent grants could easily be carried to a point where the university's own decisions on the use of the remainder of its funds would be virtually determined by the commission's decisions."[29]

Therefore the commission stated that it intended to recommend earmarked grants only in the case of costly developments such as new medical or veterinary schools.

> When such a development is recommended and approved, special additional recurrent grants will be added to the normal recurrent grants recommended for the university over the next two triennia and the university will be notified of the amounts.[30]

In considering new departments or the diversification of activities within existing departments, schools or faculties, the commission decided that earmarked grants would not be recommended but the university would be notified which of such developments were approved or disapproved. The commission definitely did not care to encourage diversification at the expense of more favorable student-staff ratios. Most of the requests which came from the universities for new departments or the improvement of old departments were approved by the commission.

The commission noted that the University of Western Australia

---

28. *Ibid.*, p. 41.
29. *Ibid.*, p. 35.
30. *Ibid.*, p. 35.

would rise to approximately 8,000 full-time and 2,000 part-time students by the middle of the 1970s. It was interesting that the university held that it should not go beyond that size if it were to keep its integrity. Moreover, the site upon which the university was built could not conveniently provide for a larger number of students. Hence, the university itself recommended the establishment of a second university in time to receive students in 1975.

The state government had come to the same conclusion. Therefore, the commission recommended that the sum of $150,000 should be added to the recurrent grants of the University of Western Australia and $50,000 to its planning grant for the triennium 1970-72.[31] This would begin the development of a new university, the site having been reserved by the state government in the metropolitan area of Perth. The commission recommended the establishment of a new medical school in South Australia and requested recurrent grants of $23,000 for 1970, $64,000 for 1971, and the same for 1972, and capital grants for planning and preparation totaling $100,000 for the triennium.

Recurrent grants recommended for 1970-72, did not include changes in academic salaries because when such changes occur, they are normally the subject of special legislation.

SUMMARY OF DATA AS BASIS FOR 1970-72 GRANTS

Table 1 presents the enrollment picture for Australian universities from 1967 to 1972 with the last three years indicating estimated enrollments.

Table 1: Total Enrollments in Australian Universities Actual 1967-69, Estimated 1970-72[32]

	Undergraduate	Graduate	Total
1967	70,513	11,651	82,164
1968	74,658	13,112	87,770
1969	80,146	14,215	94,361
1970	85,935	16,205	102,140
1971	90,730	17,645	108,375
1972	95,205	19,200	114,405

31. *Ibid.*, pp. 38 and 65.
32. *Ibid.*, pp. 15-16.

If one goes back to 1946, the Australian universities enrolled 17,066 students and this was only 2.3 percent of the population aged 17-22. Eleven years later, when the decision was being made to establish the A.U.C., enrollments had grown to 28,171. For three years, 1958-1960, the enrollment increased by an average of more than 13 percent per year. By 1962, the enrollment was 63,317 students, which was 6.8 percent of the 17-22 age group. This was nearly three times the percentage of the age group attending in 1946.

The estimate, as indicated in Table 1, is that there will be 114,405 full-time university students by 1972. That would be 9.3 percent of the population aged 17-22. If the estimates for the 1970-72 triennium hold up, graduate enrollment will have increased at a rate approximating that of undergraduate enrollment.

Table 2 indicates grants actually made for the years 1964 through 1969, and proposed grants for 1970-72, there is a chance to compare the increased support from both state and commonwealth governments. Enrollments for the triennium 1970-72 will be twenty-three

Table 2: A.U.C. and State Grants—1964-72[33]

Triennium and Type of Grant	Commonwealth Share and % of total		State Share and % of total		Total
1964-66	$000	%	$000	%	$000
Recurrent	122,629	44	157,680	56	280,309
Capital	53,685	59	37,309	41+	90,994
Research	6,000	67	3,000	33	9,000
Total	182,314	48	197,989	52	380,303
1967-69					
Recurrent	177,717	44	226,618	56	404,335
Capital	69,288	59	46,935	41	116,223
Research	3,000	42	4,084	58	7,084
Total	250,005	47	277,637	53	527,642
Rec. 1970-72					
Recurrent	235,388	44	293,939	56	529,327
Capital	75,471	59	52,448	41	127,919
Research	4,000	50	4,000	50	8,000
Total	314,859	47	350,387	53	665,246

---

33. *Ibid.*, p. 7.

percent greater than the total enrollment for the three years 1967-69. However, the recurrent grants recommended for the triennium were thirty-one percent greater than the recurrent grants for 1967-69. The eight percent difference does not include any increases for staff salaries. The increase represents a certain amount of inflation in costs other than salaries plus improvements in the curriculum and in the student-staff ratios.

Enrollment for the last year of the new triennium is expected to be 20,044 students greater than the last year (1969) of the previous triennium. To accommodate these students and to make significant improvements in the existing physical plant, A.U.C. recommended capital expenditures totaling $127,919,000 for the triennium 1970-72. These recommended grants were earmarked for very specific new buildings or the improvement of old buildings at each of the fifteen universities. Once a grant has been made for a specific building project the university is not permitted to transfer that grant to another purpose or to another fund.

CONCLUSIONS

The most significant aspect of the grants system in Australia is the unique balance between commonwealth and state support for the universities. From the beginning of the A.U.C., the commonwealth government has consistently paid forty-four percent of the operating expenditures of the universities. During the period of rapid expansion, beginning with the Murray Report, the commonwealth government has paid fifty-nine percent of capital expenditures for each of the three triennia. Commonwealth grants for research have varied from forty-two to sixty-seven percent of the total. These grants are for research and research training in contrast to grants made by the Australian Research Grants Committee which exclude the training of research workers. Although the proposed research grants for the 1970-72 triennium are pegged at $8,000,000 the responsibility divided equally between commonwealth and state governments, and may not seem adequate, it is a substantial fund when combined with the support which research is receiving from the Australian Research Grants Committee and from other agencies outside the universities. Moreover, it is significant that these funds are earmarked for research which does not increase the student-staff ratio or result in the neglect of undergraduate teaching. The Australian Universities Commission has pointed out that:

> The responsibility of the commission to encourage a national approach to university problems is beset with obvious difficulties. The commission works within the framework of university governments, state governments, and the commonwealth government, and its consistent concern is to preserve the autonomy of the university and to avoid any infringement of state rights.[34]

Australia is as large as the United States. Education is a function of local states as in the United States. Advanced education and research are indispensable to national development. For these and other reasons higher education is a national concern. However, autonomy and freedom are recognized as fundamental conditions for the effective functioning of universities. Therefore, the commonwealth government has found a way to pay approximately fifty percent of operating, research and building costs of the universities without impinging upon their autonomy and freedom.

Obviously, the success of this approach to financing universities in Australia has valid implications for the United States and the system of categorical grants by which the federal government is threatening freedom and autonomy of American universities.

The Australian success with the block-grants system is a convincing refutation to arguments advanced by Harold Dodds and others that the system will work only in a small country such as Great Britain.

APPENDIX A

Australian Agencies that Made Submission to the Murray Committee

Commonwealth agencies that made submissions included departments of air, army, defense, navy; the bureau of forestry, office of education, public service board, universities commission, ministry of labor advisory council, and the interdepartmental telecommunications advisory council.

Submissions were received from all-Australian university bodies as follows: Vice-Chancellor's Committee, federal council of university staff associations, heads of residential colleges affiliated to univer-

---

34. Australian Council for Educational Research, *Review of Education in Australia*, 1955-1962, Victoria, 1964, p. 351.

sities, National Union of Australian University Students, and professors of education.

Various administrative, faculty, staff, and student groups from each university submitted position papers and in most cases appeared before the committee for oral presentations and discussions.

Other groups that presented papers were, the Methodist Church, nuclear research foundation, ophthalmic research institute, overseas students' coordinating committee, committees on medicine, pharmaceutical society, chemical institute, social science council, Tasmanian State School Teachers' Federation, employers' federation of Victoria, institution of engineers, hospitals and charities commission, headmasters' conference, Archbishop of Sydney, chamber of manufacturers, Catholic Schools Association, Bendigo City Council, veterinary association, natives' association, institute of agricultural science, humanities research council, academy of science, atomic energy commission, Australian Council for Educational Research and several local chambers of commerce.

The above list is not complete but illustrates the response of the people to participate in the development of public policy on a problem of great concern to the total society.

References

1. Australian Universities Commission, Fourth Report. Canberra: Government Printing Office, 1969.
2. Australian Universities Commission, First and Second Reports. Canberra: Government Printing Office, 1963 and 1966.
3. Australian Research Grants Committee, Report for 1967-69. Canberra: Government Printing Office, 1969.
4. The Australian National University, Report of the Council for 1967. Canberra: Commonwealth Government Printer.
5. Australian Council for Educational Research. Review of Education in Australia, 1955-62. Victoria: Government Printing Office, 1964.
6. Burn, Barbara B. *et al. Higher Education in Nine Countries.* New York: McGraw-Hill Book Company, 1971.
7. Martin, L.H. *et al.* Tertiary Education in Australia. Vols. I, II and III. Melbourne: Government Printing Office, 1964-65.
8. Murray, Sir Keith A.H. Report of the Committee on Australian Universities. Canberra: Commonwealth Government Printer, 1957.
9. Report of the Committee of Inquiry into postgraduate education for management. Canberra: Australian Government Publishing Service, 1970.

5

Purposes, Organization, Finance, Evaluation

INTERNATIONAL PROBLEMS

The purpose of this chapter is to delineate general principles of higher education as perceived in the countries involved in this research and by authorities in the United States who have been more outspoken about our problems than they have in finding solutions to the growing crisis in higher education.

Political and educational leaders of most nations are generally in agreement on the importance of autonomy for their universities. The principle seems almost as valid in authoritarian countries as in those that are inclined toward a free society. For example, the rector of the University of Athens, in Greece, stated that his university has two functions, namely education and research. Moreover, he indicated that these are responsibilities which politicians and military leaders are unqualified to implement. He also noted that under the government dominated by the colonels, there had been no interference with the autonomy of his university to perform the two basic functions.

Dr. Antonio Pinilla, rector of the University of Lima in Peru, has engaged in extensive philosophical study of the rationale for university autonomy even under a dictatorship. He has concluded that the university with its major emphasis upon truth, both in the form of advanced education and the advancement of learning, is the repository of the greatest source of power in the contemporary world. Truth is the key to power. Where truth is permitted to flourish, unhampered by interference from governmental or ecclesiastical authorities it is possible for the university virtually to become the brain of an empire. But those leaders who become so obsessed with power that they seize the university find that they have an empty citadel. The university without freedom ceases to be a source of strength.

Although the university by the nature of its work must be free, its functions are a national concern. In studying the universities of Australia, Mr. Murray stated,

> The days when universities could live in a world apart, if ever they truly existed, are long since over. It is important that universities, in asking for help from the only sources which can sufficiently support them, keep clearly before their minds the considerations in regard to the national interest which are bound to sway governments. Any financial assistance which the commonwealth government may offer to the states or universities must stand on the base of concerted national policy.[1]

Sir John Wolfenden, chairman of the U.G.C. in Great Britain has stated:

> It is wrong, in my view at least, if a government, because it pays the piper, insists on the right to call all the tunes he plays. It is wrong, in my view at least, if universities, because they are autonomous institutions, claim the right to ignore the society which supports them.[2]

I see no contradiction in the proposition that universities must be independent and autonomous on the one hand and responsive to the needs of society on the other. Truth and freedom as advanced by responsible universities are the foundation upon which any free society must be constructed. Therefore, there is a natural partnership between higher education, the advancement of learning through research, and the improvement of any existing society.

PUBLIC POLICY VERSUS UNIVERSITY POLICY

Higher education as a function of public policy means that "Establishment interests" (the machinery and bureaucracy of universities) must give way to the general interests of society and students. No other relationship makes sense. Dimock has observed:

> Men as individuals do not usually become dangerous to the public interest so long as they are still growing in emotional maturity and living by their own abilities. If they begin to slip, however—because either their ambition has waned or they have become dissipated, or for some other reason—then they may decide to live by their wits, to become manipulators of others, to live off society instead of themselves. . . . This problem has nothing to do with political ideologies; it seems to be a universal aspect of every society, and probably always will be.[3]

---

1. Sir Keith A.H. Murray, Report of the Committee on Australian Universities. Printed and published for the Government of the Commonwealth of Australia, Canberra, 1957, p. 91.
2. Charles G. Dobbins and Calvin B.T. Lee, editors, *Whose Goals for American Higher Education?* (Washington, D.C.: American Council on Education, 1968), p. 206.
3. Marshall E. Dimock, *The New American Political Economy* (New York: Harper and Brothers, Publishers, 1962), p. 71.

Is it possible for accrediting associations to become public? Would it be reasonable to expect all the associations for higher education—those that involve boards of trustees, administrators, professors and their various disciplines, student groups, and government officials—to become public?

I believe that machinery which does not exist, at present, must be established for the protection of the public interest in higher education.

Higher education as a national concern, a fundamental thesis of every country that has advanced beyond an agrarian economy, poses questions of policies and governance. There is a clear, rational basis for the thesis that higher education is a national concern. Research reveals four major aspects of the national concern. They represent broad classifications under which all aspects of the national concern may be categorized.

The four classifications are as follows: (1) the functions of higher education; (2) organization of higher education; (3) the financial support of higher education; and (4) the evaluation of higher education.

Each of the above categories is a national concern. This indicates that boards of trustees, administrators, and faculties of universities are in no position to determine public policy on these important matters. Although no university should exercise final authority over problems affecting the total society, the solution to those problems may depend on basic and applied research carried on in universities at public expense.

In many countries of the world there is a tendency to place increasing emphasis upon higher education as a right of young people. The concomitant cost must be considered in any realistic decision regarding the extent to which the right is to be implemented.

The prime minister of Australia, in his letter to Sir Keith Murray, commissioned him to serve as chairman of a committee for studying universities of Australia and placed the whole issue of national concern in proper perspective. The prime minister requested Mr. Murray and his committee to help the Commonwealth of Australia in seeking answers to three significant questions: (1) What should the universities of Australia do? (2) How should they be organized to achieve their purposes? (3) How should they be financed?

In raising these three questions the prime minister enumerated three of the four categories of broad national concern which seem to permeate public policy in virtually all advanced countries. The remainder of this chapter represents a more detailed consideration of the four major aspects of public policy for higher education.

THE FUNCTIONS OF UNIVERSITIES

Universities must recognize the fact that they are not the only agencies of society that influence cultural development or regression. It has been noted that:

> Sinclair Lewis was one of our great educators, although he had little formal connection with institutions of higher learning and was suspicious of their cult of conformity. . . . Again and again, in his books he shows how individuals are molded not by scholastic ideals but by the mores of Main Street. He portrays universities which were like factories and taught everything from Sanskrit to beauty culture and which produced graduates who had only one ambition: to be successful.[4]

The ideas, values, mores and philosophy of the people of any civilization tend to set the tone and commitment that give substance to higher learning. Mayer has observed:

> As we look at history, we find how great teachers arose in response to the challenges of their time. Thus, because ideas and philosophy were valued in Athens, Socrates, Plato and Aristotle exerted a unique influence upon their contemporaries and upon our own time. The same was true for the Renaissance which saw an abundance of esthetic and intellectual talent because it cherished the values of the intellect. In the eighteenth century, master teachers, like Voltaire, Diderot, Holbach, were regarded as the leaders of their civilization; and in America, Jefferson was more proud of being president of the University of Virginia than of being ambassador to France.[5]

But if one takes pride in Jefferson's contribution, it is not because he was an average American. He was the genius of his era—the worthy leader of the elite as well as the masses. If he contributed to egalitarianism in America, it was because of his qualities of excellence.

The functions or purposes of any university serve as benchmarks in determining the deployment of higher education resources. Policies and purposes ought to represent a philosophical statement of the direction in which universities are to develop. Where a state or a nation supports two or more universities, it would be senseless for all

---

4. Frederick Mayer, *Creative Universities* (New York: College and University Press, 1961), pp. 26-27.
5. *Ibid.*, pp. 30-31.

of them to perform the same functions. Moreover, it would be sense-less for all of them to take on all possible university functions.

The determination of broad policies and functions of universities represents public policy rather than university policy. The distinction is absolutely indispensable to intelligent strategy and tactics by which scarce public resources are used. It has always been obvious that no university with imaginative leadership and faculties could ever have the financial resources to carry out all possible functions. The delineation of the broad functions to be served and the limita-tion upon the expansion into new functions are fundamental public issues on which the university is but one of the many publics.

The rationale for the differentiation between public and university policies is based upon the verifiable fact that all of the people within a state or a nation are affected by the consequences of higher learn-ing and by what goes on in the universities. But no university in the world has ever taken on itself the responsibility for meeting the needs of all of the people. Indeed, university enrollments around the world have been extremely limited and have tended to exclude any-where from fifty to ninety-nine percent of the college-age youth.

With increasing significance of higher learning for all people, the university leaders may be less qualified than many other groups for determining the extent to which all college-age youth should be served by education beyond the high school.

Education and Research

The broad objectives of education and research are universally accepted responsibilities of the universities. The reason for this was stated very cogently by a great scientist serving as rector of the University of Athens, who indicated that the scholar-teacher must always be engaged in seeking new knowledge and doing it jointly with his students as the most effective way for creating excitement for learning. The changing nature of society tends to increase the significance of the process of discovery compared with the accumu-lation of facts.

Education and research, as objectives of higher education, have sometimes served as a façade for justifying hundreds of useless activ-ities. There is almost a reverence for instruction and research in the universities. They have provided the necessary protection for the most useless sinecures (professors with tenure, status, salary, and positions without responsibilities) in the universities of almost every country in the world.

Eric Ashby, in his Carnegie publication "Any Person, Any Course," noted that between 1900 and 1970, there was an inestimable elevation in the importance of faculties to American Society. These factors have attracted to the profession types of people who would not have contemplated becoming professors in 1900. Ashby also stated:

> There is no doubt that the image of the profession has been somewhat tarnished by its exposure to such worldly success. In America it is not the fault of the academics themselves: . . . it is the fault of the institutions which employ them. When presidents put up the bids to hire (or to keep) a star academic, as picture dealers bid for a Picasso, even assuring the academic (as some have) that he need not be on the campus for more than one year in three, it is not an encouraging atmosphere for those hundreds of thousands of college teachers who do not fall into the Picasso class, but who do carry responsibility for teaching the undergraduates of America. That professors should be well paid is admirable. But that the inducements besides pay should be less teaching, less contact with undergraduates, less time on campus, is not admirable.

Although the teaching of students at the undergraduate level may be regarded as one of the most significant purposes of the university, much of this responsibility is relegated to teaching associates or graduate assistants who are engaged in the pursuit of advanced degrees in order that they may become professors and delegate their teaching responsibility to other teaching associates within a few years. In my research on this problem around the world, I was encouraged by the increasing tendency for public policy to mandate that senior faculty members should not make up more than a reasonable percentage of the total faculty, and that among new appointments to the faculties definite percentages were to be made among younger staff people at lower academic ranks. The principal rationale for this policy was not to save faculty salaries but to recruit young members who would be willing to devote themselves to the teaching of undergraduates rather than following their own personal research interests.

I was greatly impressed by the role of the Australian Research Grants Committee which administers some $20,000,000 of research funds annually. This committee has evolved two criteria for the approval of research projects which may emanate from individual faculty members in any university in the commonwealth. First, the proposed research must be significant to the needs and concerns of the commonwealth. Second, the individual directing the research must be judged thoroughly competent by his peers and by members of A.R.G.C. Although Australia has almost an inexhaustible need for scientists and technologists to develop the country, the research committee placed considerable emphasis upon the social sciences and the humanities.

After reviewing the policies and procedures of this committee, one must raise the question of whether or not any nation is rich enough to permit every professor to pursue his own research interest at public expense. Research in the universities as well as programs of education should be coordinated with those of all other agencies of society. Otherwise, duplication of effort and waste of scarce resources are inevitable.

> For example, firms like General Electric and IBM now spend as much annually on training and education as all but the largest universities. Bell Telephone provides as much advanced instruction in applied mathematics and electronic engineering as does any American university. The Department of Defense annually spends as much on training and education as is spent by our fifty states combined.[6]

How many boards of trustees and legislators take these facts into consideration as university research programs are funded?

Resource and Manpower Development

The exploration, utilization, and conservation of the natural resources of any nation are clearly problems of national concern on which the expertise of universities is paramount. Likewise, the problem of manpower—the discovery, education, and utilization of human talent, with consideration for the dignity of each individual and the necessity of doing the nation's work, are clearly national rather than university policies.

The agricultural and industrial development of the United States is a prime example of research and skilled manpower being applied to the economic development of the nation. As a matter of fact, technology has advanced in the United States to the point that 99.2 percent of all energy expended is mechanical energy. Agriculture has been mechanized to the point that less than 5 percent of the workers

---

6. Samuel B. Gould, *Today's Academic Condition* (New York: McGraw-Hill Book Company, 1970), p. 44.

in the United States are now engaged in agricultural activities and are producing more than enough food to feed 200,000,000 people.

The Land-Grant Act of 1862 was our first major break with trans-culturation—the transmission of European culture in America. Two acts were signed by Lincoln in 1862 that severed two of the taproots of our culture. The Land-Grant Act that brought dignity to the practical arts and the Emancipation Proclamation that ended slavery. The relationship between the two is as significant for 1972 as for 1862. Curricular reform and liberalization must accompany the extension of opportunity for higher education.

James L. Morrill, president of one of the great land-grant universities, has stated the development clearly.

> To understand fully the revolutionary impact of the 'land-grant idea' on American higher education, we must remember the conditions of those times. During most of the nineteenth century higher education in this country was modeled on the European and the British plan. Higher education was reserved for a minority, for those students who were intended for the traditional professional careers, or for young people born into families of wealth and position who were to be trained presumably for 'leadership.' Most colleges were private and sectarian, and offered a strictly limited course of classical studies oriented toward the past, not toward the needs of the future and a new and growing nation.[7]

Although the Land-Grant Act was related to the shortage of skilled manpower in the North and hence to the success of the Union army, its implications and consequences were bound up with the development of the whole nation. President Morrill notes:

> The author of the Land-Grant Act, was the son of a blacksmith and vitally interested in the farmers and mechanics and all those who must win their bread by labor.
> . . . With further help of later legislation—particularly the Hatch Act of 1887 providing for the first federal support for research, the Smith-Lever Act of 1914 authorizing the organization and support of an agricultural extension service conducted jointly by the federal government and the states through their land-grant institutions—the United States has today developed the most extensive system of higher and adult education in the world.[8]

A noted British scientist and university administrator, Lord Bowden, has declared that the Land-Grant University movement in

---

7. James Lewis Morrill, *The Ongoing State University* (Minneapolis: The University of Minnesota Press, 1960), p. 4.
8. *Ibid.*, pp. 5-6.

the United States was the most important higher education event in the century that followed 1862.

Government-sponsored Programs

The governments of virtually all nations have made demands upon the universities to perform certain services in areas of great public concern and universities have generally responded favorably in meeting these social obligations. The earmarked or categorical grant for specific purposes initiated by the government, although necessary in the national interests, should not expand to the point that governments determine a disproportionate percentage of the universities' activities. The earmarked grant to carry out specific government projects should be used as infrequently as possible. This seemed to be a concern throughout the countries involved in this research. The reason is clear,

No country with which I am familiar is so vulnerable to this danger as is the United States, because most of the federal support is for specific projects dictated by Washington.

When the National Defense Education Act was favorably reported in 1958 from the committee on Labor and Public Welfare, Senator Goldwater in his minority views made the following comment:

> This bill and the foregoing remarks of the majority remind me of an old Arabian proverb: 'If the camel once gets his nose in the tent, his body will soon follow.' If adopted, the legislation will mark the inception of aid, supervision, and ultimately control of education in this country by federal authorities.[9]

I believe that Senator Goldwater's prediction will be absolutely accurate if the federal government continues the practice of categorical grants whereby federal funds dictate university functions including many aspects of teaching and research. Professors, deans, presidents and boards of trustees will be the victims of an instrumentalism—pawns in the clutches of politicians and pressure groups.

Foss has noted the changes and how vulnerable scholars are to the financial bonanza. His statement illustrates the changes that have come about in university faculties.

---

9. Philip O. Foss and Duane W. Hill, *Politics and Policies: The Continuing Issues* (Belmont, California: Wadsworth Publishing Co., Inc., 1970), p. 119.

At this year's meeting of my professional association the corridors buzzed with loud boasts of new professional privileges and perquisites. Some told of all-salaries-paid sabbaticals every three years instead of the traditional seven; others spoke of 'summer money' that automatically raises their already not inconsiderable incomes. A favorite was the easy access to large research projects, with the fringe benefits of research assistants, streamlined equipment, and jet travel to exotic places. But the trump card in this one-upping game was invariably held by the man able to exclaim: 'And I don't have to teach undergraduates anymore'![10]

As government-dictated programs increase, freedom decreases in the university and could disappear if the trend is permitted to advance without a concerted national and university commitment to maintaining the independence and freedom of the university to determine its own internal policies, curricula and research within the framework and limitation of resources available.

The education of managers, lawyers, doctors, nurses, teachers, engineers and agriculturalists are all necessary to the maintenance of a vast array of private and public enterprises that are basic to the health and welfare of any nation. But in addition to these high level practitioners in the arts and sciences of man, it is necessary that higher education move forward on the cultural front with an appropriate emphasis upon literature, music, art, philosophy, religion, and the social sciences which need to be invoked to a much greater extent in order to understand the cultural problems of our age and to make improvements, based upon research, in all aspects of human activity.

International Obligations

Increasing involvement, commitments, and significance of international relations and responsibilities make it incumbent upon universities to provide experts to work in many areas of international relations from agriculture to diplomacy. I found this to be a particular concern even of small countries and especially those countries not noted for tremendous military power. The increasing number of international organizations, the United Nations, the World Health Organization, the International Labor Organization, and many other voluntary associations among the nations of the world will rise or fall

---

10. *Ibid.*, p. 116.

in their international and humane aspirations in proportion to the competencies of personnel provided by the member nations. Excellence must be the standard in the international arena.

Increasing numbers of students from virtually all nations are going abroad to study both at the undergraduate and graduate levels. It is imperative that universities the world over be prepared to serve these great potentials for international relations and for the cultural enrichment of every university and every country involved in this large exchange of scholars and students. There are enough foreign students in the United States alone to use up every place in six universities with 20,000 each. There are over 12,000 faculty members from foreign countries teaching in American universities and colleges. Fortunately they are distributed throughout the nation enriching the cultural activities of every state and of most universities and colleges. Each of thirty nationality groups had one-hundred or more faculty members and scholars in the United States in 1968-69.

Ecological Balance and the Quality of Life

Although scientific and technological developments in the United States have made it possible for thirty percent of our people to be engaged in educational enterprises and for more than ninety-nine percent of all energy expended to be mechanical rather than human energy, there has been an inverse result upon the quality of life and environment. The air, the water, and to a certain extent the food have all been made dangerous by the industrial complex. The potential is for every person in the United States to have virtually one-hundred mechanical slaves working for him. Unfortunately the slave-master relationship has been reversed and man is about to be enslaved by the industrial creature of his own invention. Man must not become the tool of his own inventions.

This is fundamentally a breakdown in the philosophical orientation of the leaders of the nation in both educational and governmental institutions. It is a problem of metaphysics which has tended to equate reality with the production of goods and gadgets inimical to human needs. The ends of society and of production have been lost in the means of getting rich or just getting ahead.

At the beginning of the decade of the sixties, my advanced graduate students in a seminar in academic problems, over a period of several years, concluded that a liberal education should contribute to the following specific purposes: (1) to develop in students the methods of critical inquiry and the use of the main tools of thought and expression, (2) to know and understand the dynamic arts and sciences of man, (3) to provide experiences and to encourage expression in creative activities, (4) to establish the habit of continuous scholarly growth, (5) to prepare students for productive work and effective citizenship. Stated in another way we concluded that every individual should be given the opportunity to think, to know, to create, to grow, to work and to be an effective member of the community.

At the beginning of the decade of the seventies, similar groups of advanced students in my seminar on academic problems attempted to delineate a few problems on which there is no generation gap. After considerable research and contemplation, we concluded that there are three problems from which no human being can escape at any time in his life. (1) No human being can escape from himself. (2) No human being can escape from the community of men in which he must live all his life. (3) No human being can escape from the universe or the specific environment in which he must live. Perhaps the fourth problem would have to be one of economics, but some individuals may and do choose to ignore the problem of economics. They can never escape from the other three. Another interesting principle emanating from these seminars was that all students are created educationally unequal. Policies governing curricula, grades and degrees have generally failed to accept the fact of human differences in intellect and motivation.

It is reasonable to conclude that higher education has the responsibility to develop the full potential of its students. On this I am referring to the skills and talents of each individual person. I believe that the emphasis and concentration for each individual should be upon the talents which he possesses rather than attempting to fill in talents which he does not have and which may be significant only to the specialist in academic departments representing certain disciplines.

Since the individual cannot live alone, it is imperative that we draw upon the social sciences for research, perspective, and skills which will make it possible to perfect the community of men—the ultimate goal being a worldwide community in which private and national interests are identified with the necessity of social commitment to the international community based upon respect for indigenous cultures.

The problem of the environment is a consequence of means without ends. In any culture the city is the capstone; anything beyond an agrarian community must develop villages and cities. Hence throughout history the city has been synonymous with culture. In modern times, it has become the capstone of the industrial empire. In a time when advanced learning has quantitatively reached a peak, culture, as measured by the quality of life in the cities, may have reached an all-time low.

There is a tendency the world over to emphasize humanistic objectives in the universities. There is also a fundamental inconsistency between objectives and programs. The objectives should be found in the humane disciplines—history, philosophy, literature, music, art, and religion. Science and technology should be used as a means for achieving those objectives. If this could happen in America, to say nothing of the rest of the world, our abundance of food would find its way to hungry people and there would be no hungry people; the ghetto would disappear to be replaced by beautiful landscape and attractive housing; technology, based upon intelligence and humanism, would dictate a system of transportation that would stop the slaughter on American highways; education, appropriate to the eighty percent of workers who will not be in the professions and scientific and technical occupations, would be developed; minority groups would come into their own; peace would be substituted for war and we would stop the swallowing up of our natural resources for the destruction of man. The new emphasis must be the production of better human beings to live in a better society and in a better environment.

Instruction, research, service, cultural criticism and improvement, international relations, and economic development are legitimate purposes of the university only when there is justice to the individual and to the society. The two are mutually complementary. They are not antagonists. Perhaps the greatest problem in higher education is to close the integrity gap between stated objectives on the one hand and performance on the other. Performance must be in harmony with our increasing enrollment that is drawn from all strata of society.

ORGANIZATION OF HIGHER EDUCATION

Public administrator, John M. Gaus, who served as professor at the University of Wisconsin and then at Harvard for several decades, defined organization as the "arrangement of resources and personnel for the achievement of an agreed purpose with the least friction and the greatest satisfaction to those for whom the task is performed and those engaged in performing the task." A concomitant principle of educational organization is that those who must abide by a decision should have a part in making that decision. This does not mean that every individual associated with an enterprise can participate directly in the day to day administrative decisions. However, it is possible for both internal and external policies to emanate from the broadest possible base in order that the total group affected by administrative decisions may have participated in the development of policy that guided those decisions. In commenting on university governance in the United States, Foss and Hill have declared,

> It is a curious anomaly that in the United States, which thinks of itself as the most democratic country in the world, the universities, which should be living laboratories of democracy, are probably the most undemocratic in the world. . . . The norm in their administrative organization is something like this: state universities usually provide in their charter that the governor of the state shall appoint the board of regents or trustees; this board appoints the president, who is the administrative head of the institution. The regents may or may not consult the faculty with regard to this appointment. Legally, in most cases, they are not required to do so. Legally, their power over the university and all its concerns is absolute. The president, once appointed, is answerable only to them. A wise president will consult with his faculty on the problems relative to his administration of the university's affairs, but he is not required by law to do so, being responsible only to the regents. So far as the faculty is concerned, he has the authority and the power, given the approval of the regents, to act with complete irresponsibility. . . .[11]

The trustees have total power without responsibility; the president has total responsibility without the power to carry it out; the faculty has excessive authority over academic affairs and to make the tenure of the president precarious at best. Students, in many cases, pay high tuition and fees but have no say in policies regarding their use, but recently they have demonstrated that they can close a university. Foss and Hill have said:

11. *Ibid.*, p. 114.

This institutional arrangement may be said to rest upon a 'businessman's concept' of what a university is and should be. The university is thought of as a sort of factory; the president is the manager of the factory, and his word is absolute, requiring only the approval of his board of directors (regents). According to this concept the members of the faculty are hired hands. The manager of the factory may hire or fire at will; the labor force (the faculty) is not organized as a union. The fate of the university is in the hands of one man. All he has to do is convince the regents that they should support him, and if the regents are businessmen, with the 'business-man's concept' of the university, they usually will.[12]

Business sense and managerial skills have a place in university affairs but their function is to help implement rather than to determine policies and objectives.

Students, faculties and administrators inside the university are affected by the important decisions which are made by members of the university community and all of them should be involved in the policies that guide internal decisions.

Externally, the total society, the state, and the nation are affected by the consequences of higher education. Therefore, external policies affecting the relationship between the university and the nation (and this includes the broad functions of the university as well as its external relationships with the formal organizations that support it) should be matters of *public policy*. The state, the nation and the society that support the universities, and are in turn affected by their consequences, must participate in the development of public policies that determine function, organization, finance, and evaluation of the universities.

I visited with student leaders in universities in several countries where it was easier for a student leader to see the rector or vice chancellor than it is for the dean of students to see the president in some American universities. I also found much more significant participation on the part of the faculty in determining the allocation of financial resources than obtained in most universities in the United States. The center of power in most of the universities of the world lies with the faculty which we would call the college. I believe that the faculties have far greater autonomy in Australia, New Zealand, Thailand, India, Greece, Italy, France, Germany and England and in the countries of Latin America than the corresponding schools and

---

12. *Ibid.*, p. 115.

colleges have in the United States. In no other country which I have visited is there such a proliferation of central administrative positions, layer upon layer, as found in the large state or private university in the United States.

On the other hand, it seems to me that academic departments in the United States are vested with greater authority than in any country which I have visited. This is a consequence of the developing bureaucracies at the level of schools and colleges corresponding to the hierarchy of administration at the central level.

> The principal organizational problem in higher education and of American society is to find a means by which we can achieve, in the words of Dimock, "government protection of the general, unprotected interest against selfish interests whose activities weaken the fabric of society and put in jeopardy the good life that people seek . . . . we are beginning to make some progress toward defining this crucial area of the public interest as something that must be protected. . . . Even political scientists, who supposedly are the special protectors of government and its works, have often taken the narrow and cynical view that government may legitimately be captured by interest groups; that the governmental process is a matter of access and manipulation; and that because of this jungle situation there is a constant circulation of elites, with wealth, business, labor, the military, and bureaucrats all jockeying for position.[13]

Unfortunately, universities (both public and private) have not escaped this phenomenon. Trustees, administrators, faculties, politicians, and now students (because of failure of other groups) are all in a competitive struggle for power over the academy:

> The job of the top men in any organization, private or public, is to infuse administration with such a sense of the whole that even routine activity becomes energizing to the individual. Those who work for government must have their objectives set by the public, but their duty lies in using to the fullest their individual initiative.[14]

The distance between the bottom and the top of the university hierarchy has become too great for anyone to have a sense of the whole.

> Government comes into being because people want what government is able to provide; it is the only institution capable of taking the interests of everyone into account.[15]

---

13. Dimock, *op. cit.,* pp. 63-64.
14. *Ibid.,* p. 65.
15. *Ibid.,* p.66.

And government cannot do this unless it is protected against its own selfish interests and those of pressure groups. The central idea in the Bill of Rights and the United States Constitution was to place certain hard-won human rights beyond the research of government. But this protection can be breached when government falls into the hands of selfish interests.

Academic programs in universities tend to fall completely into the hands of individual specialists. I believe that the specialists in any organization represent a centrifugal force which may bring about the disintegration of the organization. The alternative to this is strong academic leadership rather than a burgeoning bureaucracy, increasingly isolated from academic problems and more concerned with problems that affect the bureaucracy itself.

In comparison with other countries I believe that the United States has greatly overemphasized the role of boards of trustees, because we have pretended that they actually make policy that governs the university. In truth, the trustees know very little about the internal functioning of their universities. As a matter of fact, there is no one who actually knows what goes on in a large American university. Few members of boards of trustees have the expertise or the time to understand anything below the level of the central bureaucracy. The idea that boards of trustees determine what goes on within a major American university is a myth which must be exposed before a national organization can be designed. Competency, expertise and concern for the public interest rather than power and prestige should be requisites for participation in the development of policy and in the making of decisions to implement policies.

Although the private colleges and universities are in great financial difficulty and many could be forced to close, we must save these institutions from disappearance from the American scene. In doing so, we may preserve the integrity of the whole system, because of what can be learned from free universities. Seidenbaum has observed,

> A public school, such as a wing of the University of California, must answer to a chancellor and a president and a governor and a Board of Regents and a legislature and an electorate. Some of those overseers, especially the elected ones, are not exactly responsive to restructuring institutions for individual learners.
>
> A private university, of course, has its own trustees to placate and many trustees at many private schools are more obsessed with improving the physical plant than improving the life of the mind. But private university

trustees can be persuaded. Privately. They do not have to prove their political muscle in front of television cameras. They don't have frightened constituents to appease before the next election. . . . The private schools are in a position to experiment. A privileged position. They can offer the public some valuable examples to follow.[16]

I believe that it is possible to learn from the private college how important it is to distinguish between the control of universities by literary men and control by (in the words of Justice Marshall in the Dartmouth College Case of 1819) "a machine entirely subservient to the will of government." In my view, millions of dollars are being spent by our federal government to persuade higher education leaders to abandon their basic purposes, and their intellectual morality.

Autonomy Without Bureaucracy

The increasing complexity of universities around the world has mandated an increase in public support and public concern. Autonomy has been emphasized as a public trust because wise leaders in every sector of society know that a university can perform its functions only in an atmosphere of freedom. Therefore autonomy is not a right of those who work at the university. It is a privilege extended by the society as a necessary ingredient for a viable academic community.

Building up tremendously expensive public relations and propaganda offices, increasing the central administrative bureaucracy, and mobilizing trustees, alumni and citizens generally to support a bureaucratic establishment almost totally divorced from its fundamental functions is contrary to concepts of autonomy and academic freedom. In some universities individuals are working overtime in order to avoid building an inordinately large bureaucracy. In other universities individuals are working overtime to justify an increase in the same.

There is a great inconsistency among university administrators regarding the concept of autonomy. The university system which subordinates several small universities, and sometimes large ones, to a central university president depreciates the significance of autonomy except for the most prestigious university in the system. On this

16. Art Seidenbaum, *Confrontation on Campus* (Los Angeles: The Ward Ritchie Press, 1969), pp. 106-107.

point Sir John Wolfenden, former chairman of the U.G.C. in Great Britain, stated:

> I am not, as chairman of the University Grants Committee, director-general of the universities of Britain. I am often tempted to think that my job would be a great deal easier if I were. But that would be fundamentally wrong, because each university is an autonomous, chartered, responsible corporation; and the whole essence of a university's life requires that it should make its own decisions, within its known and predictable income, and determine its own priorities.[17]

Sir John concluded that he was humbly proud to be involved in an operation which combines as well as can be expected in this imperfect world, the proper autonomy of the universities and the proper degree of responsibility for the expenditure of a considerable amount of public money. Autonomy most significant to universities has been summarized by Eric Ashby who noted the following essential elements:

> (1) freedom to select students and staff and to determine the conditions under which they remain; (2) freedom to set standards and to decide to whom degrees should be awarded; (3) freedom to design the curriculum, recognizing, of course, the standards of professional bodies; (4) once having obtained external support, freedom to allocate it without being subject to further inspection; (5) and finally, the right to require nonacademics participating in governance to identify with the university and not to act as representatives of outside interests and also to delegate all academic decisions to the academics themselves.[18]

Professors have never run the universities in any nation without a certain degree of public concern and interference. But in the contemporary societies, all people are affected by what goes on in the universities. It is neither possible nor desirable to delegate this responsibility entirely to the academic community. The President of the American Council on Education, Dr. Logan Wilson, in support of conclusions of Professor W. H. Cowley has stated:

> I agree with him that—as tax-exempt, non-profit institutions—colleges and universities exist to serve the general welfare and that full control of a profession or occupation by those who practice it directly, be they teachers, lawyers, merchants, clergymen, or civil servants, would constitute syndicalism rather than democracy.[19]

---

17. Dobbins and Lee, *op. cit.*, p. 208.
18. Eric Ashby, *Universities: British, Indian, African* (London: Weidenfeld and Nicolson, 1966).
19. Dobbins and Lee, *op. cit.*, p. 135.

Mr. Wilson also noted:

For a number of years decisions made by the legislative and executive branches of government in Washington have tended to reduce the autonomy of colleges and universities by increasing the outer rather than the inner direction of higher education. A well-known medical dean recently remarked that his office controlled only $200 thousand of his total $8 million medical school budget, all the rest of the allocations being determined largely by actions in the nation's capital. And although we often think of Harvard as being a model of independence, a noted political science professor there expressed amazement at how little control even Harvard now has over Harvard.[20]

The system under which our universities now operate, which is based upon an instrumentalist national plan, is eroding away university autonomy; providing uneven, inequitable and inadequate support; and destroying public confidence in higher education.

Protection Against Political Arena

The 1915 Declaration of Principles, proclaimed by the founders of the American Association of University Professors, noted that, although professors are appointed by the university's trustees, they are not the trustees' employees, just as a federal judge appointed by the President of the United States is not the president's employee.

The university is a great and indispensable organ of the higher life of a civilized community, in the work of which the trustees hold an essential and highly honorable place, but in which the faculties hold an independent place, with quite equal responsibilities—and in relation to purely scientific and educational questions, the primary responsibility.[21]

The above quotation is in harmony with the position of the rector of the University of Athens—that colonels and politicians are not competent to direct research and education. Protection against the political arena is a paramount concern of universities everywhere in the world, because creative scholarship cannot flourish under political, religious, or any other kind of repression.

Many of the oldest universities in Latin America would rather give up government support and regress to the status of medieval monasteries than have government supervision of their activities. To a large extent this is what has happened. In making a study concerned with the reorganization of San Marcos University in 1958, I found

---

20. *Ibid.,* p. 140.
21. A.A.U.P. Bulletin, *The 1915 Declaration of Principles.* Reprinted in Spring, 1954, pp. 90-112.

that 95 percent of the members of the faculty were on part-time appointments and were earning their incomes from professions and business enterprises outside of the university—income from the university averaging only $25 per month. San Marcos prided itself on its autonomy and age. It was noted for little else.

I do not believe that the major universities of any nation in the world have surrendered as much of their autonomy to the national government in the last 25 years as the universities of the United States. For example, the Board of Trustees of Stanford University is largely dominated by executives from defense establishments such as Hewlett-Packard, Lockheed Air Craft Corporation, Northrop Aircraft, and General Dynamics.[22] The staff of the university is deeply involved in research for the department of defense, and the grants are earmarked for specific purposes dictated by the defense department.

The budget of Massachusetts Institute of Technology for research in the academic year 1967-68 was $174,000,000 and 95 percent of this came from the federal government, with $120,000,000 from the defense department alone. One noted scientist in Great Britain has called attention to the fact that the total budget of M.I.T. is nearly as large as that of all British universities combined. Of course, M.I.T. is free to reject the federal subsidy. But facilities and faculties have been increased to match the subsidy. To turn back now would leave M.I.T. in a position similar to Lockheed's financial plight of 1971. The alternatives were federal subsidy or bankruptcy, freedom or free enterprise to the contrary notwithstanding.

The defense contracts for the University of Rochester increased from a million dollars in 1966 to $13 million in 1968, the year when Rochester employed as its vice president and provost the chairman of the defense science board, which was regarded as the most important pentagon advisory committee in the area of science.[23] President Wallis of the University of Rochester has stated:

> Freedom of universities to establish their own priorities and patterns of coherence has been eroded as the importance of funds from the government has grown. . . . Grants have to be rationed in some way; and the way is necessarily formal, mechanistic, and above all uniform—in short bureaucratic in a literal, not a pejorative, sense. . . . Funds from an excessively large private source can have as unbalancing an influence as government funds; that is to say, in accomplishing their particular objectives through

22. *Look* Magazine, August 26, 1969, *The University Arsenal,* p. 34.
23. *Ibid.,* p. 35.

universities, large private agencies may diminish the autonomy and diversity of our system of higher education.[24]

Further evidence of the interdependence of major universities and the department of defense is the extent to which Pentagon officials are appointed to high administrative positions in the universities. It sometimes appears that there is more than a coincidental relationship between these appointments and Pentagon grants.

The above cases which involve prestigious, independent universities indicate the extent to which that independence is being lost. Education and research programs in virtually all of the major universities in the United States are being developed as a result of, and tailored to fit, categorical grants provided by the federal government. Purposes and programs are justified because of the availability of funds to support them. The means dominate the ends of higher education. Fundamental axiological decisions are governed by the availability of dollars.

Enrollment Quotas and the Admission of Students

The number of students to be admitted to institutions of higher learning is a matter of grave public policy. It cannot be entrusted to the universities. I found increasing evidence that public policy rather than university policy is determining the accessibility of higher education in countries around the world.

Within the enrollment limitations established for each institution, it is almost universally accepted that faculties and administrators should determine admission standards. No outside agency should dictate who should be admitted nor who should be denied admission to a university, but it does make sense for the larger public of which the university is a part to determine how many and what percentage of the youth of the nation will receive an education beyond high school. The types of institutions required and the diversity of programs, degrees and governance are significant policies.

The fundamental issue is whether each individual has a right to formal education limited only by his talents and his motivation. The decision in some countries and in some states in the United States is to make education beyond the high school available to all students. If this policy is adopted and at the same time universities and liberal arts colleges do not have curricula and programs adequate for anyone

24. Dobbins and Lee, *op. cit.*, pp. 179-181.

except those in the upper twenty percent of high school graduating classes, it will be necessary for the public to deal with alternative opportunities. Unfortunately, universities and liberal arts colleges are not noted for designing alternative opportunities for students who cannot succeed in the traditional curricula. Indeed, in many instances the leaders in universities and liberal arts colleges have opposed any measure or legislation outside of their own institutions that attempted to deal with the problem of the lower seventy-five percent.

On the basis of objective evidence, public rather than university policy must deal with the problem of increasing educational opportunity beyond the high school. The most telling evidence is the fact that approximately sixty percent who enter college never graduate. In general, the curricula were designed for an era when no more than five to ten percent of the high school graduates entered college. Now college doors have been opened to at least fifty percent of those who have graduated from high school, and they represent a broader spectrum of ability and of interest. It is neither in the interest of the individual nor of the nation for fifty percent of the high school graduates to be limited to the traditional liberal arts, professional and scientific curricula.

The community college movement may be the answer, particularly if its major emphasis includes terminal technical and vocational courses rather than the first two years toward a bachelor's degree.

THE FINANCIAL SUPPORT OF HIGHER EDUCATION

The larger public (society) should invest in higher education because society and the individual share in the economic and social increment on education. On this point Hansen *et al.,* have declared:

> The level of the price of college education and the ease of financing it are jointly relevant to individuals' decisions. An apparently high tuition rate may be quite manageable if grants or scholarships are widely available or if loans can be obtained at sufficiently low interest rates. . . . But considerations of public policy dictate that we go beyond an analysis of any individual's preferences to take account of the resources used up in the process of satisfying those preferences. This involves recognition of a socially efficient price as well as of a socially efficient set of finance terms, including an interest rate.[25]

---

25. Lee Hansen and Burton A. Weisbrod, *Benefits, Costs, and Finance of Public Higher Education* (Chicago: Markham Publishing Co., 1969), p. 89.

I agree with these authorities that society should pay a major portion of the cost; that the total cost should be paid for students whose family income falls below a certain level. This should include room, board, tuition and books for the poor people. A means test should be applied in all cases, and the cost to students and parents should be related to their income. I cannot buy the naive notion that society should pay the total cost because I am certain that the eighteen-year-old who goes to college for four to seven years benefits more than the eighteen-year-old who goes to work and pays taxes to support his cousin in college.

> This view of pricing clearly implies that society (taxpayers in general) should subsidize higher education as a matter of efficiency. Since some external benefits may be realized within local areas while others may be distributed more broadly, all levels of government—federal, state and local—would presumably share in the costs. Insofar as the bulk of external-ities accrue at the national level—in part because of population migration—this would argue for a reallocation of public financing of higher education away from state and local governments and to the federal government.[26]

In general, I believe that loans to students to finance higher educa-tion are a consequence of bills drafted by investors, bankers and lawyers who stand to gain more from government-guaranteed loans than the students or society. On this point Hansen *et al.*, noted:

> Just as there is a socially efficient price for higher education, there is also a socially efficient borrowing rate for those who cannot or prefer not to finance their education from past savings, current income, or family gifts and transfers. The capital market constitutes a device for financing educa-tion in a series of installments rather than fully at the time of purchase. The private risk (to lenders) on loans for education exceeds the social risk. As a result, education loans will tend, in the private market, to be exces-sively difficult to obtain. For the less affluent, the difficulty of borrowing to finance the costs of higher education can prove serious.[27]

It is not logical for the most affluent nation in the world to require its young people to graduate from college with thirty-year mortgages on their careers.

Solon, at the beginning of the sixth century B.C. was given abso-lute power to rule Athens, and one of his first acts was to abolish all debts that involved security of a man's person. Twenty-six centuries later we are asking students to mortgage themselves.

---

26. *Ibid.*, p. 90.
27. *Ibid.*, p. 91.

There are five major problems involving important state and national decisions in the area of finance of higher education. The first of these is the length of the planning period.

Four-Year Planning Period

One of the greatest advantages emanating from the University Grants System is the fact that it provides for a planning period ranging from three years in Australia to five years in most of the countries. The longer the planning period, it seemed to me, the more orderly university programs. If the universities know they have four or five years of operation at a certain level, it becomes possible to devote the energies of faculties and administrators to the most constructive educational and research activities.

Agencies responsible for planning legislative requests are able to collect their data more systematically, to visit universities and to study needs as expressed by faculties and administrators and to present requests for operation and buildings in which members of government can have confidence.

The year-to-year basis on which universities operate in America tends to keep the most expensive personnel constantly involved in the preparation and justification of budgetary requests. I believe that a four-year plan of financing by states and by Congress would improve the quality of higher education and reduce its cost.

Faculty and Staff Salaries and Benefits

I found practically no criticism in the various countries regarding the fact that public policy rather than individual universities should determine the level of faculty pay scales and retirement programs. If a given state is maintaining two or more universities, and there are radical differences in the pay scales for professors in the universities, I believe that some agency outside of the universities should establish the parameters and the differentiations, if any.

Where there is no policy save that established by the central bureaucracy of each university, gross inequities exist within an individual institution. I realize that the control of personnel and the budget are indispensable to institutional autonomy, but I do not believe that autonomy is threatened by public policy that would make it impossible for university officials seriously to violate the principle of equal pay for equal work. Where each university sets its own salary scales gross inequities may exist within each university and between institutions.

Scholarships, Tuition, and Fees

Public policy rather than university policy should determine the level of tuition in all state supported colleges and universities. A society cannot justify forcing a student to choose one state institution instead of another because of the difference in cost. There seems to be a greater inclination to delegate this policy to each individual institution in America than in other countries, particularly those countries that use the University Grants System. Likewise, an agency outside the universities should study the problem of scholarships and financial aid so that society itself may determine the extent to which participation in higher learning should be based upon a financial criterion.

If this policy should be left to each individual institution, the most prestigious of the state universities, as is already the case with many independent ones, would tend to develop an elitist student body based primarily upon an economic criterion.

Building Programs and Libraries

In all of the countries involved in this research, a high percentage of the cost of buildings is provided by the central or national government. I found complete agreement on the desirability of funds being earmarked for specific buildings. The U.G.C. in Great Britain provides very elaborate manuals and forms which the universities use as guides for the acquisition of sites, building requests and construction. The thing that impressed me most favorably was the extent to which the requests and needs of all universities are brought together, evaluated, and priorities established.

After observing the methodology for determining building priorities on a nationwide basis, I am convinced that there is far less subjectivity and monument building than in universities where priorities are fixed by local administrators and boards of trustees.

The most notable examples of the sharing of university support by state and national governments were in Australia, Canada, and India. These countries modeled their constitutions very much along the line of the United States combined with the British parliamentary system. In all cases education is the function of the local states. The states have played a dominant role in locating and developing the universities. The states have played dominant roles in financing the universities. Local states still provide most of the operating budgets for the universities of India.

The central government of India has used most of its support of higher education to encourage coordination and the improvement of standards. Coordination is extremely important because of the limited resources of India and the need to exercise great prudence in the use of public funds. The University Grants Commission of India enjoys great prestige and is generally reputed to have used its resources very wisely in the improvement of standards, the development of graduate programs, the improvement of libraries and in effecting a desirable degree of coordination.

Australia is an excellent example of local states extremely jealous of their prerogatives and at the same time of effective collaboration between the state and commonwealth governments in jointly supporting higher education almost on a 50-50 basis. The commonwealth support for the operating budget and the buildings is on a full three-year term and it is dependable. Earmarked or categorical grants are the exception rather than the rule.

Research leading to trienniel grants from the commonwealth government is the responsibility of an agency independent of the universities and free from government domination.

Any Plan Means No Plan

The Carnegie Commission on Higher Education has now come up with a beautiful Christmas tree for financing higher education. A federal grant to any student who needs one, a loan to any student who wants one and federal grants to institutions to make up the difference between total costs of higher education, and loans and grants to students. The ace in the hole for cartel accommodation is the grant to the institution and also the variable nature of grants and loans to students. This would be Parkinson's utopia, because the costs of higher education would increase to a point that would equal all taxes if not the total GNP within 100 years.

The same consequence would result from making grants and loans to students sufficient to pay the total costs of higher education. Costs would expand to a point equal to all available grants and loans.

The Carnegie Commission suggested augmenting federal support from $3.5 billion in 1968 to $7 billion for 1970 and $13 billion by 1976. Loans of $2,500 per year for undergraduates and $3,500 for graduate students were to be supplemented by grants to institutions of $525 for lower-division students up to $1,050 for first-year graduates and $3,500 for doctoral students. With $7,000 of support back of each doctoral student and Kerr's perennial prediction of impending disastrous shortages of Ph.D.'s plus the increased incentive for development of cadres of professional students, the Ph.D. octopus would probably replace the bald eagle as the symbol of American's might.

Kingman Brewster is being true to Yale's earliest tradition in rating the student's pecuniary status at least as important as his standing in the Congregational Church. A Las Vegas-type casino would not offer more certain dividends than for the federal government to provide or guarantee the loans and then require students to pay a percentage of their lifetime incomes. Of course, nothing is too good for Yale.

The Johnson administration proposed the Education Opportunity Bank whereby students would have created great opportunities for bankers by paying one percent of their gross income, for each $3,000 borrowed, for a period of thirty years.

Still another utopian proposal would give each person $5,000 in government credit at high school graduation or at the age of nineteen to meet expenses of a college education or for vocational training. Payment on the loan was to start at age twenty-eight.

Tax credit schemes have been proposed at the federal and state levels that would permit parents of college students to deduct college expenses from income taxes. This scheme would not help poor people, but it would be a nice bonanza for the rich, and of course nothing is too good for the poor old rich people, especially nothing in the tax structure.

Some academic administrators and one noted elder statesman on university affairs have suggested that each child be awarded the B.A. as a part of his or her birth certificate. In allowing this significant initial graduation, the emphasis could be upon education and competencies instead of degrees and grades since most employing authorities as well as criteria of standards have failed to establish any significant correlation between degrees and education or between grades and competencies. Birth and birthright would be achieved simultaneously.

Earl Cheit has reported that seven of the eight Ivy League Schools had to operate through deficit financing in 1969-70. The eighth one, Harvard, may be forced to do so in 1970-71. He concluded that all institutions are likely to be in financial difficulty if present trends continue.[28]

INCREASING DEMAND FOR REFORM IN FEDERAL SUPPORT OF HIGHER EDUCATION

Leaders in government and in voluntary associations for higher education are in substantial agreement on the need for radical changes in the process by which the federal government supports higher education. In general, they favor broad support of public and private colleges and universities. They tend to question the value of categorical grants which decrease an institution's freedom in the use of all other funds.

Representative Edith Green has urged leaders in higher education to campaign for a policy of general federal aid to higher education with as few strings attached as is politically possible. John Morse of the American Council on Education (ACE) has written:

> It is clear that if higher education is to meet its own commitments and the commitments being made in its name by the federal government, something beyond categorical aid will be required. Ways must be found to provide general institutional support.[29]
>
> The American Association of Junior Colleges (AAJC) has endorsed the principle of general institutional support to help colleges meet the operating costs of instruction and to expand educational opportunity.[30]

The American Council on Education, the National Association of State Universities and Land Grant Colleges, the American Association of State Colleges and Universities, the Association of American Universities, and the American Association for Higher Education have recommended general support of higher education either as an

---

28. Earl F. Cheit, *The New Depression in Higher Education* (New York: McGraw-Hill Book Company, 1971), pp. 152-153.
29. Educational Record, Fall of 1966, p. 43.
30. Ronald A. Wolk, *Alternative Methods of Federal Funding for Higher Education* (Berkeley: The Carnegie Commission on Higher Education, 1968), p. 56.

alternative to categorical support or as a supplement to such grants.[31]

ACE has suggested that general support go only to regionally accredited institutions; and that special grants, designed to hasten accreditation, be made to the nonaccredited colleges.

ACE has taken the lead in calling for reform in the process of financing higher education. It has stated:

> We believe the time has come for a wholesale review of the fiscal relationships between the government and higher education. It is a truism that federal programs have been enacted on an *ad hoc* basis, without a master plan or indeed without any plan at all except to meet an obvious need on a crash basis.[32]

Federal funds, according to ACE, have gravitated to a small number of universities (centers of excellence) that could come up with matching funds. This process draws funds away from regular institutional programs and results in higher costs to students to make up the deficits.

> "Compulsory cost-sharing, carried to its logical extreme, would make it impossible for institutions to engage in any research except that which attracts government support."[33]

This statement from ACE is almost identical to statements regarding earmarked grants for operation in Australia and Great Britain. As the cost-sharing grants increase, university freedom in the use of regular funds must decrease.

Some people argue that the cost of instruction should determine student fees with the government's role limited to financial assistance to students unable to meet the cost. ACE believes that the enormous expense of administering massive student aid programs makes such an approach probably the most expensive way of meeting the problem.[34]

Association of American Colleges has gone on record in favor of;

> Broad grants for instructional purposes to be expended at the direction of the institution. . . . Federal grants should be made to colleges and universities as institutions serving the general welfare . . . without discrimination between public and private institutions. Such grants should support both

---

31. *Ibid.,* p. 60.
32. *Ibid.,* p. 94.
33. *Ibid.,* p. 95.
34. *Ibid.,* p. 98.

expansion and improvement. Regional accreditation would be required for participation in ongoing grants.[35]

The Association of State Colleges and Universities and State Universities and Land-Grant Colleges have endorsed a formula that would favor the sciences, graduate work, research, and undergraduate enrollments as bases of grants. However, these associations also recommended that all types of institutions (public and private) be included.

In 1967, a panel of distinguished scholars and administrators from M.I.T., Harvard, Brown, and Syracuse universities and from the American Council of Learned Societies and the Office of Science and Technology in the Executive Office of the President recommended the establishment of the Education Opportunity Bank, mentioned earlier in this chapter.

The EOB would have loaned up to $15,000 to any student to complete his four-year degree program. The borrower would have paid for his loan over a thirty-year period at the rate of one percent of his gross income for each $3,000 borrowed.[36] If both a husband and his wife had the maximum loans, they could file a joint return and the husband would pay ten percent of their income for thirty years.

In my view, this would have been an open invitation for colleges and universities virtually to double their costs immediately. I do not believe that we should leave to the high school graduate the decision on how much he should pay for four years of education. There must be some protection against excessive charges. The same distinguished panel also concluded:

> There is little reason to think that a massive program could be better administered on a national basis by a committee than by a federal agency. (The British system works mainly because there are so few universities.) Nor is there any reason to believe that Congress would give such a committee autonomy in allocating money between institutions (and hence between congressional districts).[37]

The weakness in this reasoning is that between fifty and one-hundred federal agencies are dealing with education and with almost 3,000 colleges and universities in the United States. These experts

---

35. *Ibid.*, pp. 100-101.
36. *Ibid.*, p. 199.
37. *Ibid.*, pp. 208-209.

were right in suggesting the impossibility of having a federal agency deal directly with 3,000 colleges. But that is what Washington is attempting to do. This makes accountability impossible, and there is no assurance that the public needs are being served.

EVALUATION OF HIGHER EDUCATION

Any organization should evaluate its results with its objectives as its units of measurement. In a business enterprise the unit of measurement is the dollar because the objective is to make a profit. To an educational institution, perhaps many of the most significant results are intangible. But there are some tangible consequences of universities that can be measured.

For example, one of the tangible units of measurement which I found in other countries was the cost of a bachelor's degree. The implications of that criterion are rather astounding. The cost for each degree could include the cost for having all those students around who do not get degrees. If an institution graduates only one out of three freshmen who enter, its costs per degree could run twice as high as for the institution that graduates two out of every three freshmen who enter.

Cheit found that in a given university the annual cost per Ph.D. student enrolled in chemistry, physics and electrical engineering was five times the cost per Ph.D. student enrolled in sociology. However, the Ph.D. graduate in sociology actually costs the university fifty percent more than the cost in chemistry, physics and engineering.[38] The attrition rate in sociology made the difference.

MacGeorge Bundy has noted the reluctance of universities to use the financial statement as a clear report to the public.

> The annual financial report of the average institution of higher learning is comprehensible only to its writer, if to him. . . . Above all—and I think this is my central point—complexity is no excuse for obscurity. I have often heard colleagues in the great state universities explaining how open and complete their financial accounting has to be. I do not here question this claim, but I do make bold to suggest that they may wish to question it themselves. In their economic affairs, our colleges and universities must now become open—to themselves, to each other, to public authority, and indeed to all.[39]

38. Cheit, *op. cit.*, p. 151.
39. Dobbins and Lee, *op. cit.*, pp. 216-219.

Several years ago when I was engaged in a state-wide study of higher education in a midwestern state, I asked the business manager of a state university some questions about unit costs. His reply was to ask me "what use do you plan to make of the data? You know, costs vary in terms of the uses you plan to make of them." Francis E. Rourke and Glenn E. Brooks, in writing on the "Managerial Revolution in Higher Education," have observed,

> The defensive use of statistics is almost universal in public higher education today, and there are in fact those who feel that much of what passes for scientific fiscal management in academic administration is motivated by a desire to use fiscal data not as a real tool of university management but as window dressing designed to radiate an impression of efficiency and economy around a University's handling of its fiscal resources. . . . One midwestern institution recently found that a space-utilization study it had conducted soon became a weapon in the hands of opponents of the university's plans for building expansion, since it inevitably revealed less than full use of existing capacity. Another institution in the East avoided a similar fate only by withholding the publication of a space survey, which showed a very low rate of utilization of the university's physical plant, until it could improve its performance in this regard. Thereupon it conducted and released the findings of a new and much more favorable report.[40]

One of the problems encountered in all countries involved in this research concerned institutional research and data processing. This is a fundamental aspect of evaluation, and I believe that an agency outside of the university itself should be involved in the evaluation. Institutional research is becoming increasingly significant to each individual university everywhere in the world, but it is also important to any individual or groups who serve the government and the public in an advisory capacity concerning the level at which institutions of higher learning should be supported. Although institutional research and the gathering of data may be, for the most part, internal university responsibilities, someone or some organization must put all the pieces together in order to advise the government on the total problem of higher education within a state.

Another aspect of state-wide evaluation is the possibility of a data bank centralized by state and available to all institutions of higher learning as well as to executives and legislators in the government. Computers are extremely costly pieces of equipment, and there is tremendous prestige associated with having a computer center. There

---

40. J. Victor Baldridge, ed., *Academic Governance* (Berkeley: McCutchan Publishing Corporation, 1971), pp. 187-189.

is no doubt but what data processing equipment is necessary to teaching in a university that has complex programs in the sciences, mathematics, business administration, accounting and other fields. Expensive data-processing equipment should be used administratively only where it leads to greater efficiency and economy in management. I have advised more than one small college to return all of its I.B.M. equipment except its electric typewriters.

I have observed some business offices and registrars' offices seemingly completely computerized where personnel costs actually increased after the change to expensive data-processing equipment. In one liberal arts college, I persuaded the president to crate up and return the equipment on which the rental was $80,000 per year, and it was not necessary to make any corresponding increase in administrative and clerical personnel.

The point here is that if millions of dollars are to be spent on computers, there should be state-wide planning and utilization in order to eliminate unnecessary duplication of such expensive equipment among universities serving the same state.

It seemed to me that effective evaluation was enhanced by the longer planning period which prevailed in the countries involved in this study. There is more time for taking note of how resources have been used, and of educational consequences, where plans of operation extend over a minimum of four years into the future rather than one year.

Finally, there is abundant evidence that the evaluation of needs as well as results of universities is greatly enhanced and objectified when carried on by a commission that is independent of the universities and of the government—a commission of experts from the principal divisions of knowledge and the principal enterprises of the society.

I view accountability as a pipe dream unless there is a real balance of power in education as in government. I do not believe there can ever be any assurance of accountability as long as the education bureaucracy determines the goals, the budget and the evaluation of educational institutions. In general, I view boards of education for public schools and boards of trustees for colleges and universities as uncritical and lacking in the expertise necessary for evaluation. In far too many cases they serve as rubber stamps for central administration.

CONCLUSIONS

Broad policies and objectives of higher education effect consequences that are important to every citizen. For this reason, it is necessary that policies, purposes, programs and curricula be determined by experts from the substantive fields of knowledge combined with laymen who represent the fundamental concerns of society. We must find a way to unite knowledge with practical affairs in order to solve problems that otherwise could destroy our society.

Organizing institutions, their location, the levels of education and types of students served are matters of public policy. For example, the question of community colleges within a state must be solved not only in terms of consequences for existing four-year colleges and universities but also in terms of the consequences for students who for whatever reason cannot be admitted to, or succeed in, existing senior colleges.

It is mandatory that each state and the United States recognize the basic principle of taxing resources where the money is and using this broad source of funds to support institutions where the students are located. Equality of opportunity will remain a myth until this principle is implemented. Public policy, combining the expertise of academicians from substantive areas of knowledge and business good sense, should determine the level of financial support.

Finally, society should evaluate the product and the efficiency of the whole operation of higher education. Universities have been noted for their evaluation of most organizations in American society except the universities. Most organizations that are sincerely interested in objective evaluation know that experts from outside can make an evaluation better than those who are personally involved in the enterprise. It is now necessary for universities to learn this lesson.

References

1. A.A.U.P. Bulletin. *The 1915 Declaration of Principles.* Reprinted in Spring, 1954.
2. Ashby, Eric. *Universities: British, Indian, African.* London: Weidenfeld and Nicolson, 1966.
3. Baldridge, J. Victor, (ed.). *Academic Governance.* Berkeley, California: McCutchan Publishing Corporation, 1971.
4. Cheit, Earl F. *The New Depression in Higher Education.* New York: McGraw-Hill Book Company, 1971.
5. Dimock, Marshall E. *The American Political Economy.* New York: Harper and Brothers, Publishers, 1962.

6. Dobbins, Charles G. and Lee, Calvin B.T. (eds.). *Whose Goals for Higher Education.* American Council on Education, Washington,D.C., 1968.
7. Foss, Philip O. and Hill, Duane W. *Politics and Policies: The Continuing Issues.* Belmont, California: Wadsworth Publishing Co. Inc., 1970.
8. Gould, Samuel B. *Today's Academic Condition.* New York: McGraw-Hill Book Company, 1970.
9. Hansen, Lee and Weisbrod, Burton A. *Benefits, Costs, and Finance of Public Higher Education.* Chicago: Markham Publishing Co., 1969.
10. *Look* Magazine. "The University Arsenal." August 16, 1969.
11. Mayer, Frederick. *Creative Universities.* New York: College and University Press, 1961.
12. Morrill, James Lewis. *The Ongoing State University.* Minneapolis: The University of Minnesota Press, 1960.
13. Murray, Sir Keith A.H. *Report of the Committee on Australian Universities.* Printed and Published for the Government of the Commonwealth of Australia, Canberra, 1957.
14. Seidenbaum, Art. *Confrontation on Campus.* Los Angeles: The Ward Ritchie Press, 1969.
15. Wolk, Ronald A. *Alternative Methods of Federal Funding for Higher Education.* Berkeley: Carnegie Commission on Higher Education, 1968.

6

Principles and Plan for Federal-State Sharing of Support of Higher Education

Valid conclusions should be based upon empirical research or upon logic. The two modes of arriving at general principles are mutually complementary. They are interdependent. Each step in the empirical process must be preceded by logical hypotheses. The forward glance to perceive consequences is far more difficult than the objective viewing and analysis of a successful experiment. I do not claim empirical purity for the conclusions or principles that follow. Neither am I willing to concede that they are simply my own generalizations.

The methodology employed was a combination of inductive and deductive reasoning. Many of the generalizations are based upon specific practices that transcend international boundaries. Others are based upon apriori principles which have been in the process of validation for twenty-five centuries. For example, Plato defined a slave as someone whose purposes are dictated by another person. That generalization is as valid as ever for individuals and for institutions.

The conclusions, stated as general principles, have been in the process of formulation for twenty-five years. They are based upon direct contact with universities in many countries and on all continents. They were also influenced by my work in connection with state-wide studies of higher education in Iowa, Missouri and Kentucky.

The finance of higher education is not an exciting subject because it represents the means of the enterprise. But the means can be used to manipulate the ends of higher learning. Therefore, I went to Britain in 1962 to study the U.G.C. and how it operated to secure support without a debilitating effect upon the purposes of higher learning.

Most U.S. leaders in higher education argue that the U.G.C. idea will not work in the U.S. because we are too big and complex. Because I regard this as no more sound empirically or logically than to say the U.S. is too big and too complex for the Ten Commandments, I decided to pursue the research further.

Australia is as large as the United States and has a local state system of education including higher education. But Australia applied the U.G.C. idea and struck a 50-50 balance between commonwealth and state support of universities. They did it without destroying autonomy and freedom within the universities.

Although India is perplexed by inadequate support and standards at the local state level, the national government is using the grants system to effect coordination and improvement. Everywhere I went in Asia I heard leaders praise the integrity and accomplishments of the University Grants Commission of India.

The situation in Canada is approaching (almost paralleling) the development in Australia. Provinces organize and control the universities, but the federal government is providing almost half of the operating budgets for the universities.

The situation in the U.S. has been presented in Chapter One and to some extent in Chapter Five. Suffice it here to state that our system is not a result of any empirical research on how universities should be supported and controlled. Unfortunately, there is no evidence that the system is logical. On the contrary, I think it borders on capriciousness. By 1971, about 3,000 colleges and universities were attempting to write proposals that would fit the categorical grants from Washington. Virtually hundreds of proposals were emanating from each of the major universities. Thousands of man-years were being devoted to the writing of projects. Grantsmanship became the new profession.

Curricula, purposes, functions and philosophies have been bent, twisted, distorted and ignored in order to get in on the great bureaucratic loot. The ends of education became completely fluid—willing to flow in any direction that the means (federal funds) beckoned.

Morality, integrity, prudence, economy, efficiency, student interests, faculty concerns, national needs (outside the military and bureaucratic interests) became situational values. The distortion of goals and values permeated the independent universities to a greater extent than the state universities. Thus ended the great strength which private universities had provided for all higher education—the strength of diversity and freedom.

Generalizations that follow here represent both positive and negative aspects of systems of higher education in the United States and in other countries.

The final section of this chapter is the detailed plan for federal-state sharing of all costs for higher education in the United States. The plan is designed to be in harmony with positive principles of university autonomy combined with responsiveness to the concerns of society and individuals affected by higher learning and research.

PRINCIPLES OF HIGHER EDUCATION—AN INTERNATIONAL SYNTHESIS

1.0 Policy and Purposes.

1.1 The nature of the university demands freedom and autonomy but its functions are a national concern. This calls for a rational balance between autonomy and freedom on the one hand and responsiveness to societal and human needs on the other.

1.2 Although truth as a product of the research function of the university is the key to power in the modern world, political authorities who seize the university as a source of power soon discover that they have an empty citadel. Truth simply cannot flourish under repression.

1.3 Professors and scholars are accorded academic freedom and tenure not as license to destroy the society but as a mandate to improve it. Freedom and tenure are absolutely necessary for the advancement of truth. Repression of academic freedom could follow unionization of university faculties, because individual freedom would be sacrificed to the group.

1.4 It is imperative that leaders in government and in higher education protect and promote the public interests against impingements from special interest groups. There are approximately 20,000 special interest groups at the national level.

1.5 Higher education interests *per se* are generally special interests. Students, faculties, administrators, trustees, and alumni are all special interest groups. Individually or even collectively, they are not qualified by inclination or by competencies to determine policies for the total enterprise of higher education.

1.6 Governments may change too frequently or be too responsive to special interest groups to initiate and sustain with continuity those policies necessary for education and research.

1.7 Voluntary agencies such as associations for accreditation, land-grant colleges and universities, the American Council on Education, A.A.U.P., and foundations are special interest groups and cannot adequately determine policies for higher education.

1.8 The extension of opportunities for higher education has generally been achieved against strong opposition from the voluntary organizations, university administrators, trustees and faculties that purport to make policies for higher education.

1.9 The purposes, organization, finance and evaluation of higher education are matters of public policy rather than university policy.

1.10 Public policy advisory commissions within a state or nation should represent the substantive areas of knowledge and the principal enterprises of society. As individuals with great competencies in their fields of specialization, they must transcend their special interest groups and bring a collective judgment to bear upon policies for higher education that affect all the people.

1.11 Public policy should determine such broad purposes as what types of education will be organized and supported for what types of students; access to higher education based upon the needs of society and of individuals; the percentage of college-age groups to be provided for and alternative types of education and experiences appropriate to increasing ranges in ability among students.

1.12 Purposes, functions, programs, curricula, and research, emanating from the explosion of knowledge and technology, demand that the universities become value-oriented rather than value-neutral. The alternative to value consciousness in curricular decisions is the senseless proliferation of courses, degrees and costs of which the multiversity of the sixties was a natural and irrational consequence.

1.13 In general, it is believed that university objectives should emanate from concerns of humanity (rather than tribal interests) and that science and technology should be used as means for achieving those ends. The means of society as the means of a university may dominate the ends unless group intelligence is invoked to keep them in a logical relationship.

1.14 Democracies have tended to deify the will of the majority. In the Minnesota general assembly one finds, inscribed in marble: "The voice of the people is the voice of God." In many American institutions, and not excluding universities, this concept has been invoked to justify the most repressive treatment of minorities.

1.15 The loss of one's fundamental rights to a majority is no more acceptable than losing one's freedom to a dictator. In some respects, the tyranny of the majority is worse and more dangerous than that of the benevolent despot, the latter being somewhat easier to depose.

1.16 Universities have been used instrumentally to achieve the best and the worst of the nation's objectives. In most cases our leaders in government and in the universities have not bothered to know the difference between the two extremes. This confusion of purpose is perhaps the most serious problem in higher education.

1.17 No clear voice speaks out for higher education in the United States. In fact, more than 100 national organizations with their hundreds of regional and state counterparts represent special interest groups rather than the public concern for higher education.

1.18 On the basis of recent, as well as historical, developments in the relationship of the federal government to higher education, there have emerged certain trends which must be reversed if private and public colleges and universities are to remain open and free.

1.19 Each national crisis in higher education is approached without any long-range plan. The vacuum created by the lack of policy is an invitation for some national authority to solve the problem because of the availability of unlimited federal funds.

1.20 Fundamental purposes to be served by universities include the identification and cultivation of human talents necessary for individual self-realization and for the exploration, utilization and conservation of natural resources.

1.21 From the beginning of the first universities in the Western world, education for the professions has been a major purpose. Professionals for the health sciences, law, teaching, theology, technology, agriculture, international affairs, and for further scientific and humanistic research are all dependent upon the qualities of excellence (material, mental and moral) maintained in our universities.

2.0 The Research Function.

2.1 Research the world over is a function of universities. The rapid development of the United States in industry, agriculture, the professions and as a world power is a direct consequence of the application of basic research to the solution of economic and social problems.

2.2 Because research is of such grave significance to this nation and to all others, it must be harnessed and used to achieve humane objectives emanating from concerted public policy rather than being left to the whims of individual professors or the capriciousness of special interest groups.

2.3 Publicly supported research should be in the interest of society and should be directed by individuals of unquestioned competence. Its evaluation should be by a public group or commission of unquestioned competence from outside the research project.

2.4 All professors should be expected to engage in research related to their areas of specialization and to involve their students in the process of discovery, which may be of greater significance than the learning of the products (facts) of research.

2.5 It is hypothesized that universities can contribute more fundamentally to the solutions of problems such as urban decay, war and peace, race relations, and poverty by engaging in basic and theoretical research in substantive areas of knowledge than by initiating a whole new series of curricular entities based upon immediate, and hopefully fleeting, practical problems.

2.6 It is essential, both in terms of national concerns and individual interests, that governments recognize the fact that other agencies may be more appropriate than universities for some responsibilities in research and manpower development. This applies especially to classified research for defense and counterinsurgency.

2.7 I do not challenge the inevitability of earmarked federal grants to purchase the research deemed indispensable to the nation's defense. We do need to question whether universities are the most appropriate agencies for doing the research for the Department of Defense.

3.0 Organization of Higher Education.

3.1 Each college or university should be an autonomous corporation under its own governing board composed of fifty percent of its members from academic positions and fifty percent laymen. This is probably the only way to eliminate the dichotomy between the governing board and administration on the one hand and the faculty and students on the other.

3.2 The machinery of organization must protect the university against special interest groups in government, in society and in the university itself.

3.3 Universities have generally been organized with a central mission, commitment, or thesis. In general, they have reached the ultimate in disintegration through the centrifugal force of specialists. The function of organization and the challenge for leaders (departmental chairman, deans, vice-presidents, provosts, vice-chancellors, chancellors, presidents, etc.) is to effect a new synthesis. Otherwise, there can be no guiding policies or purposes, but only academic, student, and administrative special interests groups doing their own things in an organizational jungle resembling anarchy.

3.4 In no country that I have studied is the university so threatened by burgeoning bureaucracies as in the United States. No country that I have visited is wealthy enough to be so foolish.

3.5 University bureaucracies are, in part, a consequence of bureaucracies in government. The excessive number of agencies, bureaus, government departments and individuals controlling funds that flow from Washington to the individual universities make corresponding bureaucracies a necessity for any university that hopes to share in the federal funds.

3.6 Internally, universities must be sensitive to the relevance of expertise, concern and costs in allocating authority and responsibility. Students, faculties, administrators, trustees and other external advisory groups should influence internal policies. Students, faculties and administrators should be involved in implementing policies with administrators cast in the role of serving the ends of education and research.

3.7 American universities, noted for their contribution to the economic, political, social and military development of the United States, are less democratic than universities in most other advanced countries.

3.8 Too much power in the trustees without responsibility and too much responsibility without power in the president tend to isolate and insulate both from the faculties and students.

3.9 The pattern of administration followed in government, business and the military, when applied to a university, is absolutely inconsistent with the idea that education should encourage people to think and to act on the basis of intelligence rather than acquiescence to repression.

3.10 In most universities in the world, students have more control over their own affairs than in the United States. The same is true of faculties. These conditions are a consequence of the increasing size and complexity of the central bureaucracies that govern universities with many of the same techniques and much of the jargon, e.g., "task forces," that characterize the military establishment.

3.11 It is possible to design a system of organization for higher education that serves the public and student interests, financed by the state and federal governments on a fifty-fifty basis without being dominated by either level of government.

4.0 Private Colleges.

4.1 The growing sophistication among religious groups (apparently not so well known to the NEA and the Congress) is certain to accelerate federal support to both public and private colleges. There is no other equitable solution to the burgeoning enrollments, rising costs, scarcity of facilities, and the perpetuation of diversity which has been regarded as a strength worth saving.

4.2 Invoking the dichotomy between church and state is an antiquated gimmick. When religious freedom was a debatable condition in America, separation of church and state was a meaningful foundation upon which to build American society. But religious freedom is no longer debatable; it has been accepted by the leaders in religious and political organizations in America.

4.3 If religious freedom is a law of the land by voluntary association and agreements, then the government of the United States, including the Supreme Court, should stop acting as if the country must be protected against religion.

4.4 It is important to preserve the private as well as the public sector of higher education. Diversity has been a distinguishing characteristic of higher education in the United States. Public support can be used to preserve or to destroy private colleges. The result would be a monolithic system under political domination of the state and federal governments.

4.5 The nature of accrediting associations and of federal support (as presently administered) tend to reduce diversity and to impose conformity among private and public universities.

5.0 Financing Higher Education.

5.1 The nature of education in a democratic society precludes the dictation of curricula and programs from the federal government. The absence of a nationwide plan of support emanating from the leaders in higher education has resulted in increasing federal control of the colleges and universities of America. This came about in consequence of the fact that the federal government was called upon to bear part of the cost of higher education and the absence of a plan to keep control in the hands of governing boards, administrators, and faculties of the institutions.

5.2 The federal government must contribute part of the support for the total program rather than all of the support for parts of the program. The humanities and social sciences have been practically ignored in federal support at a time when they may be the key to survival. But the most insidious aspect of current federal support is the categorical grant which political authorities all over the world believe will destroy university freedom.

5.3 It is fundamentally wrong for a government to use finance as a weapon for dictating university purposes. When this happens, means determine ends, and a natural consequence is the crisis of purpose now so evident in America.

5.4 Financial resources should be made available to the public and private sectors of higher education to achieve humanely and philosophically determined objectives rather than as a means of determining objectives.

5.5 As government dictated programs or earmarked grants increase, university autonomy and freedom decrease.

5.6 There is an organizational and administrative vacuum in the support of higher education in the United States that borders on anarchy. It could become the graveyard of the American idea of infinite variety in advanced learning. There has been no clear vision or plan as to how to support higher education without compromising its integrity with respect both to content and to control. Present trends of government support for specialized functions in the universities will gradually reduce the freedom of both the universities and the individuals associated with them.

5.7 Congress has been inclined to determine policy at the top and to make appropriations for higher education on the basis of that policy rather than upon the basis of intelligent consideration of needs expressed by governing boards, administrators, and faculties of the colleges and universities. This is a trend which should be reversed.

5.8 Massive federal support of private universities, particularly five or six of the best known ones, is a fact that must be recognized. The principal role of these great centers of learning has been to set the tone for all higher education. They have been the private universities, made secure in their freedom by the respected Dartmouth College case. But what the Jeffersonian Republicans could not absorb through legislation or through the courts is rapidly capitulating to the power of the United States Treasury, and the whole scheme of political duplicity is clothed in the euphonious façade that the universities must remain free.

5.9 Many of our greatest universities, both public and private, get most of their support from the federal government because they do what government agencies prescribe. But British universities get seventy-five percent of their budgets from the British Treasury and do what their faculties and administrators believe they should do.

5.10 Although national interests and concerns play a paramount role in university functions, the power of federal financing should not be used to persuade or hire universities to abandon programs they know to be right and to take up research and activities they know to be wrong just because federal funds are available.

5.11 Categorial grants to universities are almost universally a response to special interest groups that have neither the expertise nor the public commitment to determine university policies.

5.12 The national concern is for adequate support of a balanced program in higher education designed to improve academic posture in the humanities and social sciences as well as in the biological and physical sciences and in the professional schools so necessary to the future of society.

6.0 Advisory Council.

6.1 Any state or nation that supports two or more universities needs an advisory agency, council, or commission to keep the government informed on university aspirations, needs and costs, and to keep the universities fully aware of the concerns of the public or society that must be considered in long-range university development.

6.2 An advisory council should not be the lackey of government nor the uncritical spokesman for universities. It should serve as a bridge or intermediary to bring together the resources and needs of higher education. It should spare university leaders the necessity of entering the political arena to secure funds and spare political authorities the awesome task of evaluating uncoordinated budgetary requests from colleges and universities.

6.3 There is unquestioned evidence that university planning and governmental support are more effective and more economical when based upon a period of four or five years rather than on a yearly basis.

6.4 Pay scales and other personnel benefits should be on a state-wide basis rather than an uncoordinated institutional plan. Unless an objective approach is used in these areas of faculty and staff concerns, universities are apt to be unionized.

6.5 Tuition, fees, and scholarships should be determined on a state-wide basis rather than by institution. Statewide policies should be administered within each institution with maximum latitude and autonomy.

6.6 Building grants should be earmarked for specific buildings. They should be based upon objective studies of space utilization and projected.

6.7 Australia, India and Canada have validated the principle that national governments can contribute to the support of operating budgets of higher education, where education is a local state function, without interfering with fundamental university purposes.

6.8 Evaluation of higher education and the determination of acceptable unit costs are two of the most difficult (and for the most part unresolved) problems for the decade of the seventies.

6.9 Institutional research carried on from within universities, and evaluated from without by an objective group (apart from the universities and apart from government) is absolutely necessary if we are to close the accountability gap.

The foregoing principles are the foundation for the recommended plan that now follows. They should serve as guidelines for establishing a viable plan and making it work.

The guidelines, or principles, I believe, safeguard the interests of students, society, the universities and colleges, and those who must pay the bill for higher education.

FIFTY STATE COUNCILS ON HIGHER EDUCATION

The existing approaches to financing colleges and universities in the United States have placed higher education in a state of anarchy. Costs have increased more rapidly than enrollment or the GNP. Tuition and other student fees have gone so high that the admission of students would be based upon an economic criterion except for the loans now available to the needy. Moreover, many authorities do not believe that it is fair to students to ask them to assume long-term indebtedness in a time of great inflation, record GNP, and consequent low purchasing power of the dollar.

Local states, legally responsible for education at all levels, are rapidly approaching the limits of their taxing power for higher education. At the same time states are being asked to assume a higher percent of the cost of elementary and secondary schools because the local property tax has run its course as a source of school revenue. Now it is being challenged on constitutional grounds because of the gross inequities in educational opportunity which it has perpetuated throughout our history.

The federal government is probably the only hope for financing higher education without resorting to regressive taxes and tuition charges and repressive admission standards based upon ability to pay rather than ability to learn. The federal government has no legal mandate to accept the responsibility but it has the moral obligation and constitutional right to do so.

The absence of any legal responsibility has caused the federal government to exact a very high price for its financial contribution to universities. I believe that the price exacted has been the loss of autonomy and freedom within the universities—and these are the very qualities that made advanced learning and research indispensable to the national welfare in the first place.

Careful consideration of the plight of private as well as public institutions of higher learning in the United States, the increasing costs of physical facilities, laboratory, and library resources, administrative and academic personnel, and the rising costs to the student all mandate the reappraisal of the whole haphazard approach to the finance of higher education.

The overhead costs, administrative personnel, public relations and development offices, and other bureaucratic establishments in the colleges and universities are absolutely astounding in the proportion of the higher education budget which they consume, compared with the overhead cost of maintaining the University Grants Committee which secures seventy-five percent of the budget of British universities.

The above conditions, together with America's desire to keep the control of education decentralized, form the backdrop and the rationale for the scheme herein proposed. Another aspect of the rationale is the fact that almost every state is concerned about the coordination of public higher education, and in some cases, of all higher education, in order to approach this increasingly complex problem with the maximum utilization of limited resources.

ONE COUNCIL FOR EACH STATE

The proposed plan would include a Council on Higher Education in each of the fifty states. The number of members should be sixteen plus a full-time chairman. An executive secretary and small secretariat would need to be full-time employees working under the chairman or administrative head of the council. Titles such as chancellor, president, commissioner, or director should be scrupulously avoided. All such titles imply administrative authority over higher education absolutely inimical to the success of the council and of higher education.

The council should be composed of an equal number from the substantive areas of knowledge and the principal aspects of American society. Membership on the council should be drawn from the academic disciplines and professions including the humanities, natural sciences, social sciences, medicine, engineering, education, and from representatives of the cultural, business, industrial, and agricultural society in which higher education operates. The academicians on the committee would be drawn from the colleges and universities of the state, representing the most distinguished professors and possibly certain deans of colleges, but excluding central administrators of the colleges and universities who would present budgetary requests to the council.

The council would be an advisory agency, not a governing body. Governing boards of colleges and universities would continue their existing functions. The coordinating function requires the best judgment of professionals from the sciences, humanities, social sciences, professions, business, and industry. With the exception of a small research staff, the members should serve without pay, excepting the allowance necessary for the expense of attending meetings.

METHOD OF APPOINTMENT

Initially, the sixteen part-time members of the council should be appointed to terms ranging from one to eight years. After the initial appointments, two members would be appointed each year to serve eight-year terms.

Academic members of the council in each state would be nominated by the college and university presidents operating as a group. In each case, the presidents would nominate two or more people for each vacancy. The governor should make the appointments subject to the approval of the legislature. College presidents and the governor would be mandated by law to maintain a balance between representatives of academic disciplines and also among the broad cultural and economic enterprises of the state and nation.

In appointing the original lay members and in replacing them, the governor should invite nominations from the college presidents, the chief justice of the State Supreme Court, the state superintendent of public instruction and from governing boards of public and private colleges and universities. Once the council is in operation, it should be invited to suggest names to the governor for vacancies in its membership.

Under the plan herein recommended, no governor would be permitted to appoint more than eight of the seventeen members during a four-year term. Vacancies that occur in addition to the eight required to be replaced, should be filled by the remaining members of the council.

The chairman of the council should be recommended by the council itself and appointed by the governor. His first term of office should be for three to five years. Then the chairman, upon the recommendation of the council and approval of the governor, may be appointed for an indeterminate period.

Francis Wayland, president of Brown University from 1827-1855, stated criteria for trustees of a university that seem most appropriate for a state council. He noted:

Its corporation should therefore be men who are incapable of acting from fear, favor, or affection. In all official acts, they should look with equal eye upon the merits of the nearest relative, and those of a stranger. They should know no parties either in politics or religion.[1]

METHODS OF OPERATION

Members of the council should represent higher education as a whole. Each member, including those who come from universities and colleges, should be committed to serving higher education rather than looking after his own institution. I believe that there are individuals in the academic community who would gladly accept such a role. It is in keeping with the traditions of every scholarly discipline.

Almost every university has observed laymen among its trustees who could see the major problems of society and help to relate the university to problems and challenges that transcend partisan interests.

Keeping the total interests of higher education before the council would mandate concerted council and legislative effort in meeting the fundamental needs of society and students. Out of intelligent consideration on the part of experts from the basic branches of knowledge and distinguished laymen from society would emerge public policies in which the governor, legislature and citizens could have confidence. Financial support adequate for higher education to meet its responsibilities would follow as a natural result.

At least half of the members of the council should visit each institution during each planning period in order to secure first-hand data on how budgetary allocations are being used and to understand requests for improvement, expansion and buildings.

Requests for all institutions of higher learning, including community colleges, private colleges, state colleges, and universities, after careful consideration and approval by the governing board of each institution, would be submitted to this council. The requests would indicate programs to be supported, the necessary costs, and sources of income, including tuition, fees, grants, and endowments. The chairman and executive secretary of the council would be responsible for submitting a coordinated budget to the bureau of the budget and the legislature in each state.

---

1. Richard Hofstadter and Wilson Smith, *American Higher Education: A Documentary History,* volume I (Chicago: The University of Chicago Press, 1961), p. 343.

The council would advise the government on higher education needs and keep universities fully aware of the concerns of citizens and government officials. But no requests for higher education appropriations should be submitted to the legislature except through the council. Moreover, the four-year grant for higher education should go to the council as a block grant for operating budgets, research and buildings. Distribution to individual institutions should be made by the council.

Building grants should be for specific buildings based upon institutional requests and justification emanating from research data pertaining to utilization of physical facilities.

Grants for undergraduate and graduate teaching, and for research should be specifically categorized and any transfers from one of these major categories to another should require prior approval of the council.

The portion of the total cost of higher education to be met by each state legislature would be fifty percent. State appropriations could be made on an annual or a biennial basis, but commitments should be made for four years as a planning and implementation period.

Support would be provided for both public and private institutions. The precedent for this policy has been firmly established. The difference in this proposal is that regular operating budgets would be supported which should protect the autonomy of both private and public sectors.

The secretariat operating in each state would engage in institutional research involving costs, facilities, personnel, enrollment, program development and evaluation. Each legislature should require a constant study of costs at different levels of higher education in order to approach the problem of appropriations objectively and without discrimination against any institutions.

I believe that the cost of research in each institution, where it is paid for by the state or federal government should be carefully reviewed by the council, and grants for research should be known to institutions and to the public. Criteria that should determine each grant should be the significance of the research and the competence of the researcher to complete the project. It should not be taken for granted that all professors automatically spend one-half time in research.

The council should evaluate completed research projects. For this and other purposes, the council should have the authority to appoint *ad hoc* committees to perform specific tasks such as the evaluation of research in progress as well as projects that have been completed.

The fifty chairmen of the Councils on Higher Education should present a quadrennial request to the United States Commission on Higher Education to supplement institutional and state legislative funds for each state. The federal appropriation would be made on a four-year basis and the commission would distribute funds directly to the Council on Higher Education of each state for distribution to the institutions. Individual colleges and universities would have no direct contact with the federal government. The U.S Commission would perform the function of presenting the case for higher education to the federal government.

THE U.S. COMMISSION ON HIGHER EDUCATION

The United States Commission on Higher Education should be appointed by the president of the United States. It should consist of a full-time chairman and fourteen part-time members.

One half of the members should be appointed from academic disciplines broadly representative of the major divisions of knowledge with particular emphasis upon the sciences, humanities, social sciences, health sciences, education, technology, and research.

The other half of the members should represent the major enterprises of American society. Both lay and academic members should be drawn from the geographic regions of the United States but without regard to political entities.

The chairman and all other members should be selected with the same care as a Supreme Court Justice and should serve for terms of five years with three members to be replaced or reappointed each year.

The chairman, and executive secretary and a small staff would represent the full-time Washington staff. The commissioner of education or an associate commissioner for higher education should serve as adviser to the commission and provide research data to assist the commission in gaining a complete understanding of national needs for higher education and resources necessary to meet those needs.

The major task of the commission would be the preparation of the four-year request for grants to higher education. During the third year of each quadrennium, the commission would need to invite the chairman and executive secretary of each state council to present four-year requests for operating budgets, buildings and research. These hearings would take a minimum of fifty days.

Commission members and subcommittees appointed by the commission would need to visit different states and meet with each state council once during each four-year period as a part of the preparation for the next quadrennium and to evaluate procedures and results of federal-state sharing of the total responsibility for higher education.

Four-year grants by the fifty states and the federal government should be announced six months prior to the end of the previous four-year grants.

Grants from the federal government should provide fifty percent of all operating costs for both undergraduate and graduate programs of instruction and a full fifty percent of research and building costs. What is indicated here is federal-state sharing, on a 50-50 basis, of all costs above the amount provided by tuition, fees and endowments. The level of cost for operating budgets, research and buildings would be determined by the state councils and the U.S. Commission on Higher Education. There should be no open-ended (Pentagon-like) approach to costs.

The unit of cost for undergraduate and graduate programs could be the cost of producing different types of degrees, thereby eliminating any advantage to the institution that enrolls a higher proportion of students destined to attrition out before earning any degree.

On the other hand, a more acceptable unit of cost would be based upon the number of students enrolled at different levels from freshmen to Ph.D. candidates. In this case, state councils should determine general admission standards.

Any institution that wanted to increase costs beyond those levels determined by state councils and the U.S. Commission would be on its own in doing so. However, tuition and fees in public colleges and universities in each state would be fixed at a uniform level by the state council.

There is no argument here to make costs uniform among states or even within a given state. Indeed, I believe that costs should vary within a state and within a given institution, e.g., between departments. But I think such variations should be justified by institutional research and data carefully weighed and evaluated by each state council which would make state and federal allocations to each institution.

ADVISORY FUNCTIONS OF STATE COUNCILS ON HIGHER EDUCATION

In general the council in each state would advise colleges and universities on the public concerns and needs for all types of higher education. Of equal importance would be the council's advice to state and (through the U.S. Commission) federal governments on institutional development and support adequate to state, national, and student needs.

Specific Advisory Functions

1. Quotas of students for whom higher education should be provided.
2. Types of institutions necessary to meet state needs.
3. Location and functions of any new institutions of higher learning.
4. Unit costs for different levels and types of education.
5. Salary levels for both academic and staff personnel.
6. Percentages of academic personnel at different levels or ranks.
7. Relative importance in terms of budget for teaching and research.
8. Extent to which teaching associates may be used to teach undergraduates.
9. Scholarships and criteria for their allocation.
10. Specific building programs to be funded by state and federal governments and their costs.
11. Curricular development, particularly where new departments or schools are to be created within existing institutions.
12. Degree programs by institution in order to achieve coverage of basic areas of knowledge with a minimum of duplication.
13. Development of comprehensive community colleges.
14. The number, location and support of medical and other professional schools.
15. Presentation of four-year higher education budgetary requests to state legislatures and to the U.S. Commission on Higher Education.
16. The allocation of state and federal funds to individual institutions.

The sixteen points enumerated above are matters of public policy that cannot be determined by the governing boards of individual institutions unless a state is so rich as to be oblivious to costs. These public policies illustrate the coordinating function of state councils. Moreover, this approach spares the governor and legislators the painful responsibility of serving as referees for colleges and universities competing in the political arena.

Items 15 and 16 above are matters on which state councils go beyond the advisory function. They must be the only avenue by which budgetary requests go to the government and by which government funds are allocated to centers of higher learning.

CONCLUSIONS

The University Grants Committee has functioned effectively in Great Britain because the program has been as decentralized in administration and control as if England were as large as the United States. The United States Government, in its administration of federal funds for higher education, has followed a centralized policy as if the whole nation were as small as the state of Rhode Island.

If the principle of decentralization is valid in a nation that is smaller geographically than one of fifty American states, then only adminstrative and educational ineptness could ever persuade the people of the United States to adopt any policy for higher education based upon centralization of control in Washington.

Under present conditions, we have about 3,000 institutions at the state level that deal directly with the federal government on research grants, loans, scholarships, and building programs. The number of separate applications would be greatly in excess of the number of institutions involved because schools, colleges, departments, and individuals within each institution apply directly to various federal agencies for grants and research funds.

At the Washington level, the situation is equally confused because at least fifty major federal agencies, without any coordination, are involved as sources of funds available to colleges and universities. The expense, inefficiency, and waste of governmental and educational talent, operating through 3,000 project trails leading to Washington and more than fifty leading from Washington to the colleges, illustrate the ultimate in planned chaos.

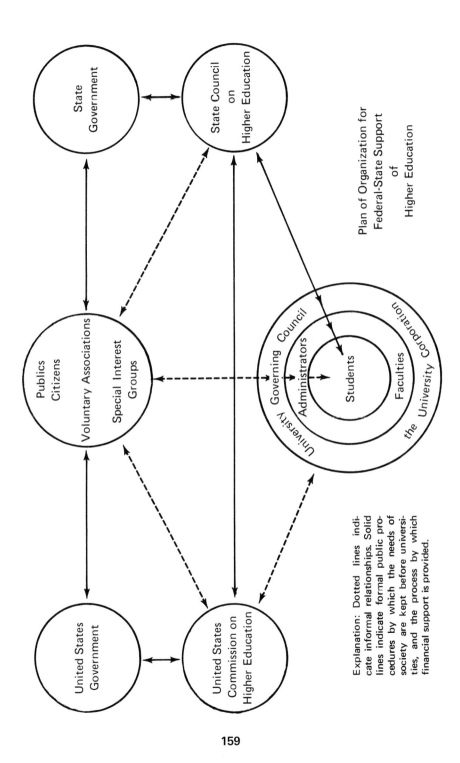

Plan of Organization for
Federal-State Support
of
Higher Education

Explanation: Dotted lines indicate informal relationships. Solid lines indicate formal public procedures by which the needs of society are kept before universities, and the process by which financial support is provided.

State Government

State Council on Higher Education

Publics
Citizens
Voluntary Associations
Special Interest Groups

University Governing Council
Administrators
Students
Faculties
the University Corporation

United States Government

United States Commission on Higher Education

This scheme proposed for the United States would change the 3,000 project trails leading to Washington to a maximum of fifty carefully marked channels, and these would narrow to one broad avenue to federal funds, the Bureau of the Budget. Moreover, there would be only one agency through which federal funds would be distributed to higher education—the U.S. Commission for Higher Education—which would coordinate requests from the fifty states and distribute grants to the fifty state councils on higher education.

Most Americans who have observed the University Grants System in Great Britain conclude that it would not work in the United States. Reasons stated are generally related to differences in the two countries on the basis of physical size, college enrollments, costs of higher education, and America's infinite variety in systems of education. In general, the arguments are no more convincing than if they were to state that representative government will not work in America because it works in England.

The most important part of the research for the proposal in this chapter was carried out in Australia. In that country, education is a function of local states, but, as reported earlier, there is a 50-50 sharing between commonwealth and state governments of the costs for higher education.

Although the universities under the University Grants System of Great Britain enroll fewer students than do the colleges and universities in one of our larger states, the British Government believes that it would be impossible in terms of efficiency and economy in administration and disastrous from the viewpoint of integrity in research, teaching, and learning in the universities to attempt centralization of control in London.

If no such system, appropriately modified, will work in the United States, there are causes more basic than the differences in the size of the two countries, the differences in the number and size of the universities, the differences in the availability of higher education, and the differences in the size of the budgets for higher education.

Philosophers, scientists, humanists, theologians and political statesmen have, throughout history, recognized the universal nature of certain values. America has benefited from a rich heritage in religion, education and government. But there is an accountability gap between promise and performance in higher education. It involves purposes, organization, finance, and evaluation. The concerns of youth and of society make it imperative that the accountability gaps be closed. State legislators and members of Congress have the responsibility to initiate legislation to provide public policy that will promote the public interest.

References

1. Educational Record. *Fall of 1966 and Fall of 1970.* American Council on Education, Washington, D.C.
2. Hofstadter, Richard, and Smith, Wilson. *American Higher Education: A Documentary History,* Volume I. Chicago: The University of Chicago Press, 1961.
3. Wolk, Ronald A. *Alternative Methods of Federal Funding for Higher Education.* The Carnegie Commission on Higher Education, Berkeley.

About the Author

Raymond Gibson was raised on a farm in Kentucky. He taught a one-room school at age eighteen and was president of the Duluth State College in Minnesota eighteen years later.

Two college degrees were earned at Western Kentucky University and the Ph.D. at the University of Wisconsin where he pursued an interdisciplinary program in educational administration, history and philosophy of education and public administration.

Professor Gibson spent ten years in public school administration in Kentucky and Wisconsin and three years in business prior to going to Wisconsin. He was engaged in international education for five years, serving as director of the Point Four Program in Peru from 1950-52; then he served as director of the Education Mission Branch of the U.S. Office of Education from 1952-55.

In 1953, the author spent one semester in Thailand and wrote a critical evaluation of education at all levels for the minister of education. The two key recommendations of the study were: (1) the creation of a department of teacher education in the ministry of education and (2) the development of a modern degree-granting teachers' college in Bangkok. Both of those recommendations were implemented by Supreme Decrees issued by the king of Thailand.

In 1953, the author advised the minister of education in Saigon on the location and organization of a teachers' college in Saigon. When he returned to Saigon three years later, there were 1,600 students on the campus of the new teachers' college.

In 1956, Professor Gibson was invited to return to Thailand to spend a semester studying the reorganization of Chulalongkorn University, and in 1958, he was invited to return to Peru as guest of the Peruvian Government to study the reorganization of San Marcos University in Lima. On that visit, the Peruvian Government awarded the Distinguished Service Medal to the author.

On another trip to Peru, he served as consultant to the rector and board of trustees on the development of the University of Lima.

At Indiana University since 1955, the author organized the department of higher education in 1958—a department that has graduated over 200 doctoral graduates. They hold administrative and teaching positions in every type of institution of higher learning.

During the years at Indiana, Professor Gibson has served as consultant to twelve different college presidents and as a member of the board of trustees of a private college. He was the United States representative to a UNESCO-sponsored world conference on higher education in Latin America held in San Jose, Costa Rica in 1966. He directed a statewide study on the Resources and Needs for Higher Education in Iowa in 1959-60, and served as chairman of a team of three consultants who did a statewide study on the Expansion and Coordination of Higher Education in Missouri in 1962. In 1965, the author served as a member of a survey team on The Growth and Development of Higher Education in Kentucky.

Finally, during the summer of 1972, the author served as coordinator of a group of consultants from Western Kentucky University working at the University of Austral in Valdivia, Chile. This program was sponsored by the Inter-American Development Bank.